THE ZOO TOURIST

Visiting America's Zoos and Aquariums

by Lenny Flank

Red and Black Publishers, Florida

© Copyright 2021 by Red and Black Publishers

All photos by Author

Contents

Introduction: Noah's Ark in the 21st Century   5

Zoos
Philadelphia Zoo, Philadelphia PA   13
Central Park Zoo, New York NY   19
San Diego Zoo, San Diego CA   25
Columbus Zoo, Columbus OH   31
Smithsonian National Zoo   37
Bronx Zoo, New York NY   45
Busch Gardens, Tampa FL   51
Disney's Animal Kingdom, Orlando FL   57
San Antonio Zoo, San Antonio TX   63
Brookfield Zoo, Chicago IL   69
Dallas Zoo, Dallas TX   75
Zoo Atlanta, Atlanta GA   81
Zoo Miami, Miami FL   87
Los Angeles Zoo, Los Angeles, CA   93
Zoo Tampa, Tampa FL   99
Houston Zoo, Houston, TX   105
Denver Zoo, Denver CO   111
Cincinnati Zoo, Cincinnati OH   117
Pittsburgh Zoo, Pittsburgh PA   123
Oklahoma City Zoo, Oklahoma City OK   129
Kansas City Zoo, Kansas City MO   135
Lehigh Valley Zoo, Allentown PA   141

Aquariums
Monterey Aquarium, San Francisco CA   147

Sea World, Orlando FL, San Diego CA, San Antonio TX   153
Shedd Aquarium, Chicago IL   159
New England Aquarium, Boston MA   165
Georgia Aquarium, Atlanta GA   171
Aquarium of the Pacific, Long Beach CA   177
Clearwater Marine Aquarium, Clearwater FL   183

Photo Album   189

INTRODUCTION

Noah's Ark in the 21st Century

The first "Zoos" were called *menageries*. These were simple collections of caged animals, especially exotic species from faraway provinces, gathered together by kings and emperors to show off their power and wealth. The earliest of these discovered so far is at Hierakonpolis, Egypt, where in 3500 BCE the Pharaohs kept a collection of Hippos, Elephants, Baboons and Hartebeests. King Nebuchednezzar kept a royal menagerie in Babylon, and the Chinese King Wen of Chou maintained a private animal collection called the "Garden of Intelligence". Alexander the Great sent back animal specimens from his Asian conquests, which were displayed in Athens. The Roman Emperors not only imported exotic animals from all over the known world for use in the arena games, but also for large private collections that showed off the extent of their exotic provinces as an example of Rome's power in bringing civilization to the barbarian world.

Royal menageries were especially popular in medieval Europe. The most famous of these was the royal collection at the Tower of London, gathered in the year 1204 by King John I from animals that had been given to him as gifts by diplomats and ambassadors. The caged Lions, Bears and Leopards were maintained for the amusement of the royal family.

When Queen Elizabeth I ascended to the throne in 1558, the Royal Menagerie at the Tower of London was opened to the public. By the 1700's, the collection had expanded to include Polar Bears, Kangaroos and Ostriches, and members of the public could see the animals for an admission of one and a half pence, or if they brought a cat or dog with which to feed the Lions. In 1765, the menagerie of the Austrian Emperor at Vienna's Schonbrunn Palace was opened to the public, as was the French royal animal collection at the Jardin de Plantes in Paris in 1795.

By the beginning of the 19th century, political revolutions had begun to wipe away monarchy as a governmental system, and science and the study of the natural world had swept across Europe and would soon produce the Industrial Revolution. In keeping with the new democratic worldview, governments in Europe began transforming the "royal menageries" into publicly-owned "zoological gardens" as a way of gathering the world's animals into places where they could be academically studied, as well as providing entertainment and curiosity for the public. In 1828, the newly-formed London Zoological Society opened the London Zoo in Regents Park (though it was not fully available to the public until 1847), and followed with a public Aquarium in 1853. The London Zoo became the prototype for the publicly-owned (usually by a nonprofit Zoological society) zoological park. The Dublin Zoo opened in 1831, and the Melbourne Zoo in Australia in 1860. The Philadelphia Zoological Society was established in 1859, but the Zoo itself, delayed by the Civil War, was not opened until 1874; meanwhile the Central Park Zoo in New York City was opened in 1864—leading to both Zoos claiming the title of "America's First Zoo".

These early zoological parks were not much different in appearance from the royal menageries. The animals were confined in small iron-bar cages akin to prison cells. Some of them were taught to perform tricks for the public, who threw them bits of food as a reward. Because knowledge of animal care was lacking, most of the animals died after a short time, and had to be regularly re-established by collecting trips that gathered replacements from the wild. Zoos tended towards "postage-stamp collections", vying with each other to exhibit one example of as many different species as possible—the more exotic, the better. The underlying message was that of the "conquest" of the primitive natural world by "civilization" and "progress"—the same message that had been broadcast millennia earlier by the Roman Emperors with their menageries.

But in the early 20th century, Zoo design underwent a major revolution, led by one man—German animal collector Carl Hagenbeck. In 1907, Hagenbeck founded a Zoo in Hamburg that was vastly different from anything else in the world. The iron-bar prison cells were gone: moats and ditches replaced walls and fences. Hagenbeck housed his animals in large open areas that were landscaped to mimic as much as possible the natural habitats in which they were found. These enclosures contained a mixture of different species, living together as they would in the wild. And rather than being housed together according to taxonomic groups, with all the "mammals" here and all the "reptiles" there, Hagenbeck organized his Zoo along natural geographical lines, with the Asian animals in one section and the African in another. By the 1930's, with the appearance of the automobile, Hagenbeck's open-air concept had become transformed into the "safari park", where animals were displayed in open fields with dirt roadways where cars could be driven. The first of these "safaris" opened in Whipsnade Park in England in 1931.

During the political and social turmoil of the 1960's, the environmentalist movement rose to prominence, and Zoos came under heavy criticism. They were, critics charged, "animal prisons", where living creatures were confined in substandard cages as objects of amusement and spectacle. These criticisms were all valid, and in response, "Zoos" underwent a major transformation, led largely by the Jersey Zoo in England, the Bronx Zoo in New York, the Woodland Park Zoo in Seattle, and the Brookfield Zoo in Chicago. The iron-bar cells disappeared, the fenced pens were removed, the "Monkey Houses" were torn down—replaced by Hagenbeck's vision of open-air naturalistic enclosures which replicate the natural environment as closely as possible, and which allows for the free-roaming mixing of different species that would be living together in the wild. Emphasis on replicating nature has now led most Zoos to be partitioned by geography rather than taxonomy—instead of seeing zebras in one area and Rhinos in another, now one can see zebras, antelope, Rhinos and wildebeest all together in large open areas replicating the African Plains, as they would live in the wild. They are even able to have predators and prey seemingly intermingled with each other, safely separated by barriers that are invisible to human visitors.

The purpose of the Zoo also changed completely—now it was no longer about simply displaying as many different varieties of species as possible for the public. The watchwords for every Zoo became "education" and "conservation". Zoos would become lifeboats for all the species that were rapidly disappearing from the wild, places where endangered and threatened species could be bred to augment their dwindling numbers, where we could learn as much as possible about their needs, both in captivity and in the wild, so we could increase their populations and release captive-bred animals back into the wild, make their lives as comfortable, stimulating, and enriching as possible while doing so, and at the same time educate the public about the entire issue of endangered and threatened habitats. Zoological societies began establishing research stations around the world to study natural habitats, both to learn how to protect them, and how to prepare their captive-bred animals to survive in them.

In the US, the Association of Zoos and Aquariums (AZA) was set up as a nationwide accrediting agency, which produced minimum acceptable standards regarding animal housing and care (AZA produces its own updated Animal Care Manuals for Zoo species, specifying the acceptable housing and care requirements), financial responsibility and transparency, conservation work, veterinary care, and staff training. Every Zoo that applies for AZA membership undergoes a multi-day inspection by an outside team of Zoo experts, and members are required to be re-certified every five years. All of the major Zoos in the US are AZA-accredited.

AZA (with its overseas counterparts) also coordinates breeding and exchange programs between Zoos through international "Species Survival Plans (SSP)", which are drawn up for each species to facilitate the best genetic matches between Zoo animals for breeding the most robust population for release back to the wild. As a result of their focus on captive breeding for re-release, the number of species on display in most Zoos has now become smaller, but the number of individuals for each species has increased as breeding groups became important, and particular Zoos have became specialized in captive-breeding a small number of species for conservation and release. Today, the goals of every modern Zoo are conservation, captive-breeding, and education.

And Zoos have been remarkably successful in meeting those goals. A growing number of species, including California Condor, Pere David's Deer, Guam Kingfisher, and Przewalski's Horse, are already virtually (or completely) extinct in the wild and survive only in Zoos, which are breeding them to maintain the population until wild areas can be re-established for them to be introduced back into. Many Zoos do rescue and rehabilitation work for injured or orphaned wild animals: the Monterey Aquarium in California does rescue work with endangered Sea Otters, and the Zoo Tampa in Florida has a specially-built hospital for treating rescued Manatees. Working together, Zoos have also founded a "frozen Zoo", in which multiple DNA samples from endangered species are permanently stored in liquid nitrogen as an insurance policy against extinction, allowing future biologists to re-create the species from cloned DNA.

By the 2010s, many Zoos and Aquariums had expanded their educational programs to include more interaction with the animals. "Touch tanks" allowed people to gently pet Stingrays, small Sharks, and Sea Stars. "Feeding stations" allowed Zoo-goers to feed lettuce or carrots to animals like Giraffes or Rhinos, while behind-the-scenes "animal encounters" allowed small groups of visitors, accompanied by a zookeeper, to pet and touch animals like Tortoises, Rhinos, Capybaras, or Sloths and see them up-close. All of these programs encourage people to become more directly involved with the Zoo and the animals they keep.

Problems and valid criticisms remain, however. The most trenchant criticism is directed at keeping highly-intelligent and wide-ranging social animals in captivity. Many animals live sedentary lives and have needs that can be easily provided in a Zoo. In the wild, for instance, an arboreal Tarantula would be making its silk shelter on a tree trunk or a rockface, and would never venture more than four or five inches away from it. In a glass tank at the local Zoo, its life is utterly no different than it would be if it were in the wilds of Panama. The same is true for snakes in their rock shelters, turtles in their ponds, or Prairie Dogs and Meerkats in their dens. Animals like these really don't know or care whether they are in captivity or in the wild, as long as their requirements are met.

But that is emphatically *not* the case for large intelligent species, particularly social ones, like great apes or Elephants or Orcas or Dolphins, which live in extensive social groups and also require enormously large territories and constant social interaction and intellectual stimulation. While Zoos try their best to provide these needs, with large outdoors enclosures and "enrichment" in their environments, nearly all fail. Indeed, a number of Zoos are now giving up their Elephant and great ape colonies simply because they lack the physical space and/or resources to meet those needs.

But here is the dilemma: these "charismatic megafauna" are precisely the animals that people are willing to pay to see. Few people are willing to pay to see spiders and turtles, but lots of people are willing to pay to see Orcas and Elephants and Pandas—and Zoos must be sensitive to that economic reality, even if, as a nonprofit organization, the Zoological society is not driven by a profit motive. The very best educational conservation program in the world is useless if nobody comes to see it. So, the only way for a Zoo to entice people to come see it (and pay to support it) is with displays that undermine the very goal of that education.

Many Zoo educational programs attempt to solve the dilemma by using animals for talks and display that have been rescued from injury and now simply cannot be returned to the wild. That works even for Dolphins and Orcas. But it doesn't work for Elephants or Gorillas. And even the recovered rescue is still essentially doomed to life in captivity.

Some people will emphasize one side of that dilemma, some people will emphasize the other. But there is no solution for the dilemma itself, and *anything* done is, by definition, a compromise.

There are some in the US who therefore criticize the very idea of Zoos, who think no animals should ever be kept in captivity, and who declare all Zoos should be closed down and the animals "released back to the wild". As an environmentalist who has been active since the 70's with groups like Greenpeace, Earth First! and Sierra Club (and who, in full disclosure, has a membership at the local Zoo in Tampa and has visited every major Zoo and Aquarium in the US and most of the smaller ones), I must disagree strongly.

The ideal solution would of course be to leave the animals in the wild and stop cutting down and paving over all their habitats. And I'd be all in favor of that. (Indeed, I sometimes think it's the *humans* who should live in the cages, to protect the rest of nature from the madly destructive bipedal apes.) Sadly, though, that simply will not happen, at least not for the foreseeable future. Whether we like it or not (and I don't), the sad reality is that there is virtually no "wild" left anymore, anywhere. There's not one square foot anywhere on the Earth's surface that is not impacted for better or worse by humans and our activities. The entire planet is now basically one huge managed nature reserve.

Even the most extensive "natural parks" or "wildlife preserves" on the planet are still just fenced-in enclosures, albeit very large ones. And as the Elephants and Lions and Tigers in Africa and Asia who get shot every day for leaving the parks and entering the surrounding human farmlands show, even the most enormous fenced-in cage is still just a cage, and animals who leave it do so at their peril. So even the remaining "wild" animals can't be "wild". Their behavior is constrained, continuously, merely by our human ever-presence. For better or worse, this planet is ours, and everything else lives here merely because we haven't (yet) decided to wipe it out.

Given the choice of "animals in managed care" or "no animals at all", then, I don't think there's any real choice.

But there is another reason for Zoos that is, to me, even more compelling. In our urbanized world, most people see only cement and glass, and the only "wildlife" they see is Squirrels and Pigeons. We as a species have utterly lost touch with the natural world, and know none of it. And that presents an enormous problem for environmentalists. As Greenpeace is always so fond of saying, we protect only what we love, we love only what we understand, and we do not understand what we never see.

Zoos provide that opportunity. They are a place for people to see and appreciate things they would never see otherwise, in a way that photos or YouTube videos cannot. And from that appreciation comes understanding, love, and protection. When I visit Zoos, I often watch the expression on the faces of all the children there. And nobody who has ever once seen the look of amazement that passes over the face of a child who has seen a live Rhino or Ostrich or Tiger up close for the first time, can ever again doubt that it leads precisely to the desire to protect all of those living things and the places where they live, which is the sole basis for any successful environmental movement. Scratch any active environmentalist, and you will find someone underneath who probably spent a lot of time in the Zoo as a kid.

So join me as I take you on a tour and tell you the history behind some of the most interesting Zoos and Aquariums in the US.

PHILADELPHIA ZOO
Philadelphia PA

In the early years of the American republic, Philadelphia, as the second-largest city with a population over half a million, was the country's intellectual, educational, and social capitol. It is therefore no surprise that the city was a center of scientific study, establishing a large number of universities, medical schools, and scientific institutes. Early in the 19th century, Philadelphia resident Benjamin Franklin had raised the idea of a public zoological garden in the city, and when President Thomas Jefferson dispatched the Lewis and Clark expedition into the newly-purchased Louisiana Territory in 1804, one of its goals was to discover what kinds of animal life lived in the region (Jefferson was reportedly hopeful that the expedition might find still-living Mammoths in the unexplored interior).

After the London Zoo opened to the public in 1847, ideas began to circulate about creating a similar Zoological park in the United States. In Philadelphia, this cause was taken up by William Camac, a local doctor. On March 21, 1859, the Pennsylvania State Legislature voted to issue a charter establishing a nonprofit Philadelphia Zoological Society, with Camac as its president, for the purpose of raising public and private funds to establish a Zoo in the city. It was the first zoological society in the United States (and today the Zoo still claims the title "America's First Zoo").

When the Civil War broke out in 1861, however, plans for a Zoo had to be put on hold. It wasn't until the 1870's that post-war Philadelphia was finally able to begin devoting money to public works again. The Zoological Society was given 30 acres of land in Fairmount Park, along Girard Avenue, at the site of "The Solitude", the riverside manor house built in 1784 by William Penn's grandson John, who had moved to England and left the home empty. It became a part of the Zoo grounds. (Later, the Zoo was extended to 42 acres.)

The Zoo was enclosed by a stone fence, and the Victorian stone facade columns and wrought-iron gateway, designed by local architect Frank Furness, still stand today.

The Philadelphia Zoo opened to the public on July 1, 1874. On opening day, 3,000 people paid an admission price of 25 cents for adults and 10 cents for children. Visitors could also purchase a yearly Zoo membership for $10, and a lifetime membership for $50.

The original display consisted of 616 animals, including bears, deer, leopards, monkeys, bison, wolves, birds, and an Indian Elephant. Some of these had been collected in Africa and Asia by the Smithsonian Institution, which had not yet completed construction of its own National Zoo in Washington DC and loaned its animals to Philadelphia in the meantime. The new Zoo was served by its own railroad station, and also by its own dock on the nearby Schuylkill River, with ferry boats arriving every fifteen minutes. In its first year of operation, the Zoo attracted 228,000 visitors—almost half the city's population.

The Zoo quickly expanded its collection, but because of its geographically small area, the Philadelphia Zoo was slow to adopt the Hagenbeck system of moated outdoor enclosures, and housed most of its animals in stone-facade Victorian-style buildings. The Bird House was opened in 1916, followed by the Elephant House in 1941 and the Carnivore House in 1951.

From the beginning, the Philadelphia Zoo made efforts to breed its animals and take a scientific approach to their care—

something not many other Zoos were doing at the time. The first successful births at the Zoo were Red Deer and White-Tail Deer born in 1874. The Zoo was also the place for the first captive births in the US of a Chimpanzee and an Orangutan (both in 1928), the first captive-born Cheetahs in the world (in 1956), and the first Echidna bred in North America (in 1983). In 1901, Philadelphia became the first Zoo in the world to build a dedicated on-site animal care veterinary center, which was still in use over 100 years later. Researchers here developed a special diet for captive Flamingos, then in 1935 Zoo employee Dr Ellen Corson-White developed the first specially-formulated foods for other Zoo animals (called "Zoocakes").

In 1938, the first Children's Zoo in the US opened in Philadelphia, where young kids could see farm animals like Cows and Horses, and could feed and pet Goats, Sheep and Ducks. The Children's Zoo has since been remodeled and updated several times.

In 1976, the Philadelphia Zoo began to move away from its previous "postage-stamp collection" philosophy, and began to actively concentrate on education and conservation. The collection shrank from over 3000 individuals, most kept alone, to around 1300, most of which are now kept in breeding groups. The Zoo no longer keeps Elephants since there is not enough space for a proper paddock for them.

The Zoo's new Mission Statement emphasized "educating the public about exotic animals, promoting and participating in worldwide conservation efforts for endangered wildlife, and providing exceptional recreational opportunities for families". An Education Department was established, which began a series of outreach programs for children, including The Treehouse exhibit (built in the original Giraffe Barn), the Rare Animal Conservation Center, and the Footprints program to educate people about the effects of global warming. A series of new open-air enclosures were also constructed to replace the old buildings: the African Plains (opened 1975), Bear Country (opened 1980), and Carnivore Kingdom (opened 1992).

In 1995, a fire broke out in the "World of Primates" building which killed 23 animals, including Gorillas,

Orangutans, Gibbons, and Lemurs. As a result, the 2.5 acre open-air Primate Reserve replaced the "monkey house". To make maximum use of their limited space, the Philadelphia Zoo has been a pioneer in the use of pathways and elevated "climbing trails" that allow animals like apes, monkeys and big cats to move around the Zoo, from one enclosure to another. These trails lead to drinking pools, resting places, or sheltered spots, and encourage the animals to move around in their environment much as they would in the wild.

The Zoo also began a number of captive-breeding and conservation projects. In 1996, Philadelphia became the first Zoo in the US to exhibit endangered Giant River Otters from South America, and soon became the first Zoo in the world to successfully breed them, starting in 2004. In the new Avian Center, the Zoo keeps and breeds two bird species, the Guam Rail and the Guam Kingfisher, that are now extinct in the wild.

The Guam Kingfisher, *Todiramphus cinnamominus cinnamominus*, is the largest of the three Kingfisher subspecies that are found in the Pacific. It is found only on the island of Guam. Although they are brightly colored with blue backs (the males have cinnamon-colored bellies and heads while the females are cream-colored), they are shy birds who tend to spend most of their time on the ground at the edge of forests, hunting for small lizards and insects. Breeding pairs will nest in cavities that they excavate together in dead trees or in abandoned termite mounds.

During the Second World War, US Marines invaded Guam and established an important military base there. As a result, large amounts of military supplies and equipment began to flood into the island from other bases in the Pacific. And that resulted in an ecological disaster. Hidden away in some of those shipments were stowaway Brown Tree Snakes. This is a large arboreal snake about six feet long, with mild venom, that preys almost exclusively on birds. By the 1950's, a breeding population of snakes had become established on Guam, and in the absence of their natural predators, they quickly expanded to cover the whole island. Since there were no native snakes on Guam, the local bird species had not evolved any defenses to them, and the Brown Tree Snakes soon began depleting the bird populations. One of the hardest hit was the Guam Kingfisher—the voracious snakes ate both the adult birds and their eggs.

By 1984, there were only 29 Guam Kingfishers left on their native island, and the birds were listed as a critically endangered species. It was decided by the US Fish and Wildlife Service to capture all of the remaining birds to protect them, and captive-breed them to increase their numbers for release later. A number of captive birds are being bred on Guam itself, but it was decided that keeping all the birds in one place made them too vulnerable to a disease outbreak or accident, so the birds were distributed amongst several different Zoos in separate parts of the US (a concept known as an "assurance colony"). By 2020, captive breeding at the Philadelphia Zoo, the Lincoln Park Zoo, and others, under the Guam Bird Rescue Project, had increased the Kingfisher population to 130 individuals. Meanwhile, the Fish and Wildlife Service was trying to eliminate the non-native Brown Tree Snake and establish a protected refuge in the areas of remaining habitat that can be rendered snake-free. So far, however, there has been no large-scale reintroduction of Guam Kingfishers, and the birds are extinct in the wild. They survive only in Zoos.

In addition to its breeding work with the Guam Kingfisher, the Philadelphia Zoo has also joined with a number of global partners to help carry out other conservation efforts around the world. In Brazil, the Zoological Society is helping the *Associação Mico-Leão-Dourado* (Golden Lion Tamarin Association) to educate local people about the need to protect the Tamarins and to encourage local farmers to set aside areas where the Tamarins are living. The Zoo has also formed programs with Amphibian Ark and the Amphibian Survival Alliance to captive-breed endangered frogs from Haiti and Ecuador. In Ecuador, the Philadelphia Zoo is working with the local Zoo at Amaru to protect local habitat and establish breeding programs for endangered amphibians. To help save the frogs in Haiti, the Philadelphia Zoo's reptile department now keeps over 1400 individuals from ten endangered species at its care center in the US, where, working with biologists from Port Au Prince, it has successfully bred nine of these species.

In 2013, conservation biologists from the Zoo traveled to the tiny islands of Mauritius, in the Indian Ocean, to bring back a number of critically endangered Rodrigues Fruit Bats for study and breeding. It is estimated that fewer than 100 of these bats remain in the wild.

Other Zoo projects involve partnerships with Polar Bears International to protect and preserve Polar Bear habitat, the Ongava Research Center which studies and protects Namibian Lions, and the Tuanan Orangutan Research Project and Sumatran Orangutan Conservation Program to protect Orangutans in Indonesia. Locally, the Zoo also works with Philadelphia conservation groups and city officials to help restore and protect native bird habitat in Fairmount Park.

The Philadelphia Zoo gets about 1.2 million visitors per year.

CENTRAL PARK ZOO
New York NY

Just before the Civil War, New York was the largest city in the US. To enhance its reputation as an international cultural center, the city decided to duplicate the expansive public parks that were found in London and Paris, and in 1853, the state legislature authorized the city to obtain 700 acres of land in the center of Manhattan for use as a public park and common space, under the management of an appointed Parks Commission. The selected area was low-lying and swampy, with large rock outcroppings scattered around. After evicting some 1600 people living there, including German farmers, Irish pig-keepers, and a small African-American community, "Central Park" was established in 1857. In 1862, additional land was obtained which expanded it to its current 843 acres.

There was no Zoo in the original plans for the park, but by 1859 an informal animal collection had appeared anyway, made up of various animals donated to the Park by local residents, including some swans and ducks, a Porcupine, a Raccoon, three Bald Eagles, several Cockatoos, a young Alligator, and a bear cub that was left with a startled city employee as the Park was being constructed. These animal gifts were later housed in a building on Fifth Avenue and watched over by a disabled Civil War veteran.

The city decided to expand this impromptu collection and turn it into a permanent zoological exhibit, and in 1861 the state legislature authorized 60 acres of the Park to be earmarked "for the establishment of a zoological garden" (although in the end only 6 acres were actually set aside for the Zoo). A formal charter for the "Central Park Menagerie" was issued in 1864, with local resident William Conklin as its Director. The Zoo was first planned for the spot where the American Museum of Natural History is now located, but during the Civil War it was placed near the Arsenal, where it remains today. A number of Victorian-style stone buildings were constructed to house the animals. Today, the Central Park Zoo claims the title "America's First Zoo"—a title it still disputes with the Philadelphia Zoo, which was chartered in 1859 but did not actually open until after the Central Park Zoo did.

The Zoo's collection quickly grew. Telegraph inventor Samuel Morse donated money and a collection of animals. General George Custer donated a Rattlesnake, and Civil War General William T Sherman donated three African Cape Buffalo that his troops had captured from a menagerie in Georgia. A pair of donated South American Peccaries produced the first offspring to be captive-born at the Zoo, in 1866. Over 250 animals were obtained in the Zoo's first two years.

William Snyder, who had worked with the Ringling Brothers Circus as an Elephant trainer, became the Zoo's lead animal keeper, and he began a program of exchanging animals with other Zoos. Snyder also obtained the Zoo's first Indian Elephant, named Hattie, from Carl Hagenbeck. By 1873 some 3000 people a day were visiting the Zoo, and this increased to 8000 a day by 1902.

In 1874, the *New York Herald* newspaper ran a story on its front page declaring that dozens of animals, including Lions, Rhinos and Leopards, had escaped from their cages at the Zoo and were rampaging through the city, with 49 citizens already dead and over 200 injured while National Guard units had been called out to kill the beasts. As the story's very last paragraph revealed, it was a hoax—or, more politely, a satire, written by a staffer who said that he had seen a Leopard "almost escape" while being transferred to its cage at the Zoo, and he wanted to call attention to what he considered unsafe conditions with "a harmless little hoax, with just enough semblance of reality to give a salutary warning." Residents who didn't read all the way to the end of the article were panicked—many locked themselves inside and waited for the terror to end. The "Central Park Menagerie Escape Hoax" became one of the most notorious media pranks of the 19th century.

In 1934, the city, at the urging of Parks Commissioner Robert Moses, decided that the small buildings and cramped cages were inadequate, and applied to the Federal Government for funds to rebuild the entire Zoo, using money and workers from the WPA (the Depression-era government works program). The new buildings were cutting-edge for their time. The center of the new layout was the Sea Lion Pool, which was an open-air enclosure designed by local architect Charles Schmieder, who took the then-unusual step of actually studying the habits of wild Sea Lions to try to duplicate their conditions as closely as possible. The Sea Lion Pool is still in use today. Other buildings, with larger more spacious cages, were laid in a rectangle around the pool. These were designed by architect Aymar Embury II, who had just finished designing the Triborough and Henry Hudson Bridges.

The reconstructed Zoo re-opened in December 1934, after just eight months of work, in a ceremony in which former New York Governor Alfred E Smith, who lived across the street from Central Park, was designated as an honorary zookeeper. The Parks Commission announced that emphasis would now be placed on displaying healthy animals in cleaner and more humane conditions.

But despite these good intentions, budgetary problems plagued the Zoo and conditions steadily worsened over time through benign neglect. By the 1950's, wealthy residents of nearby Fifth Avenue were complaining about the noise and smell that was coming from the Zoo. In 1961, a Children's Zoo was added with Pigs, Llamas, Ducks, Chickens and Penguins, funded by a donation from Senator Herbert Lehman, but by the mid-1960's the entire Zoo was outdated, squalid and substandard, and became the target of public criticism. Even the new head of the Parks Commission, Gordon Davis, called it "a Riker's Island for animals".

Finally, in 1980, the Central Park Menagerie (along with the smaller Queens Zoo and Prospect Park Zoo) was transferred from the city's Parks Commission to the nonprofit New York Zoological Society, which already managed the Bronx Zoo. The menagerie was closed down for another complete rebuild, funded in large part by a donation from *Readers Digest* publisher Lila Acheson Wallace. The Sea Lion Pool was expanded and the Polar Bears were given a new enclosure, but it was decided that there was no room for a proper enclosure for Elephants, Bears or Rhinos, and these animals were all given to other Zoos. The rectangular layout of the Zoo was kept, but now each building was redesigned by architect Kevin Roche (whose credits included the Metropolitan Museum of Art and the United Nations Towers). The Bird House became the new Zoo gift shop, and the Monkey House became the Zoo School educational center. The new animal enclosures were organized within different areas grouped by ecosystems, with the remaining old barred cells replaced by spacious glass or open-fronted habitats. In all, some $35 million was spent on the reconstruction.

In August 1988, after five years of work, the new facility opened as the "Central Park Zoo". Its naturalistic exhibits featured the new Sea Lion Pool as well as a rebuilt Polar Bear habitat and a Japanese Snow Monkey island. (The Sea Lions and the Polar Bears are the only two species that have been in the Zoo continuously from its founding in 1864.) To help pay for the construction costs and to provide a steady source of funding for the Zoo, an admission fee of $1.00 for adults and $0.25 for children was charged (up to then the menagerie had always been free to the public).

Since then, the Zoo, despite its limited space, has added two more features. The Children's Zoo was expanded and updated in 1997, and in 2009 the Snow Leopard Exhibit was opened, with three Leopards that had been transferred from the Bronx Zoo.

The Central Park Zoo receives about 1 million visitors per year. Because of its small size, the Zoo functions solely as an exhibit, with the aim of "Connecting People to Wild Nature". The Zoo is managed by the Wildlife Conservation Society (formerly known as the New York Zoological Society), which does most of its captive breeding and conservation work through the Bronx Zoo.

SAN DIEGO ZOO
San Diego CA

When the Panama Canal opened in 1914, the city of San Diego, California, population 74,000, saw an opportunity. As the nearest major port in the US for ships that passed through the Canal, the city government decided to put on a trade exhibition that would highlight the city's location and entice new businesses to locate there. As a result, the "Panama-California International Exposition" opened in Balboa Park in March 1915, as a celebration of the opening of the Panama Canal. The Exposition featured a number of exhibits and trade booths from various companies, and also had an indoor botany collection of tropical plants and an outdoor display of caged animals from North and South America. It was so successful that it added another year to its schedule, finally closing in January 1917.

Among the people who were involved with setting up the Exposition was San Diego resident Dr Harry Wegeforth, a surgeon originally from Maryland. Inspired by the success of the Exposition, Dr Wegeforth made plans to open a permanent Zoo in the city, and organized the nonprofit Zoological Society of San Diego, modeled on the New York Zoological Society. Dr Wegeforth was the Society's first President. He was joined by his brother Paul, who was also a surgeon, by Dr JC Thompson, a Navy Commander with an interest in herpteology and entomology, Dr Fred Baker, president of the City Council, and Frank Stephens, a mammologist and board member at the San Diego Natural History Society. The Zoological Society was chartered in November 1916.

The fledgling Zoo received an unexpected bonus right from the start. When the Panama-California Exposition closed in 1917, some of the nations that had sent live animals to be displayed now refused to allow them to re-enter their home country without a quarantine, and since San Diego had no quarantine facilities, they were marooned in their cages. The Zoological Society therefore adopted all of these animals, as well as a collection of Lions, Bears, Jackals, and Monkeys from the bankrupt Wonderland Zoo in nearby Ocean Beach. A short time later the Society received its first public donation—a Kodiak Bear cub named "Caesar" who was being kept as a mascot on the US Navy ship *Nanshan*. Other donations followed: a Badger, two Lynxes, a Grey Fox, a Coyote, two Golden Eagles, and some Geese.

The Zoological Society quickly raised $1,000 and its membership grew to 120 people, but it struggled to keep pace with the $100 it needed to spend each month on salary, food and maintenance for the animal collection. In 1917, the owner of the *San Diego Sun*, WH Porterfield, began to use his newspaper to promote the Zoological Society, sponsoring a contest to raise money, and forming a partnership with a local circus that made visiting children a member in the Junior Zoological Society and donated a portion of each admission to the Zoo.

In 1921, the city of San Diego donated 150 acres of land in Balboa Park as a permanent home for a public Zoo, on the agreement that the city would own the Zoo and the Zoological Society would manage it. The San Diego Zoo opened to the public in 1922.

The Zoo's first director was famed animal collector Frank Buck, but he didn't get along with Wegeforth and soon left. After a number of other people also came and went, the Zoological Society appointed the Zoo's bookkeeper, Belle Benchley, as Zoo Director in 1925. She was the first (and for many decades the only) female Zoo director in the world, serving until 1953.

From the beginning, the San Diego Zoo kept its animals in open moated enclosures and grottos. The moated Lion exhibit was the first of its kind, and the Zoo also had an outdoor Mountain Goat display (with artificial cliffs) and grottos for the Bears. In addition, the Zoo inherited the botanical garden from the Panama Exposition, which is still on public display. In 1923, two Asian Elephants were brought to the Zoo, by Frank Buck. They were named "Queenie" and "Empress". That same year, an indoor Aviary was built.

In 1926, the Zoo began running bus tours which carried visitors around the 100 acres of exhibits. They became immensely popular, and still continue today. The Zoological Society also placed emphasis on wildlife research, opening a Zoological Hospital in 1927, and carrying out field research on wild Elephant Seals in partnership with the government of Mexico and the US Fish and Wildlife Service in 1929.

In 1955, the San Diego Zoo began what would become a long relationship with television, when the TV show *Zoorama* began filming on location at the Zoo. Hosted by local TV news reporter Bob Dale, the show focused on animals at the Zoo and in the wild. Originally begun as a local show, *Zoorama* was then broadcast nationally on CBS until 1970, when it went into syndication.

In the 1960's, in response to the environmental movement, the San Diego Zoo increased its research programs. In 1969, the Zoological Society began funding the Darwin Research Center on the Galapagos Islands, and in 1975 the Center for Reproduction of Endangered Species (later renamed Conservation and Research for Endangered Species) was established. One of its first tasks was to form a "frozen Zoo" by collecting sperm and eggs from hundreds of endangered species and storing them permanently in liquid nitrogen. In 2009 the CRES was expanded again and renamed the Institute for Conservation Research.

Today, the Institute for Conservation Research is one of the leading conservation and wildlife organizations in the world. Field and lab research is carried out in the areas of animal and plant ecology, genetics, wildlife disease, captive breeding and reproductive physiology, and animal behavior. Partnerships in 35 nations help carry out field work and large-scale protection of wildlife habitats, and the Institute's education and outreach programs bring students into the lab and also offer programs for student field research. Almost 150 endangered species are studied and captive-bred.

One of the San Diego Zoos most successful conservation programs has focused on the California Condor. *Gymnogyps californicus*, a member of the vulture family, is the largest bird in North America and one of the largest in the world, with a wingspan of nearly ten feet. Historically, it ranged along the California coast and across the southwestern United States, where it nested on cliff faces and large trees and made its living by eating carrion from dead animals. Like all vultures, the Condor has a naked featherless head and neck to allow it to poke inside the body cavities of dead carcasses. Although awkward and ungainly on the ground, the Condor is a superb flyer, able to ride thermal currents and glide effortlessly for miles at a time, looking for carrion.

The Condor population had already begun to decline by the 1920's. Many of the birds were shot by ranchers in the mistaken belief that they attacked sheep or young cattle. The birds were also hurt by the decline in large North American mammals, such as Bison, Elk and Antelope, that provided much of their food. By 1940 there were no Condors outside of California. In the 1960's, the birds were devestated by the effects of the insecticide DDT, which was sprayed on fields and ingested by herbivorous mammals where it concentrated in their tissues; when the Condors ate their flesh, the DDT caused the birds to produce abnormally thin eggshells which then broke, crippling reproduction. The insecticide was soon banned, but the birds continued to decline. In 1967 they were placed on the Federal endangered species list. By 1975 they were nearly extinct.

In 1982, there were only a few dozen Condors left alive, and the US Fish and Wildlife Service concluded that the only way to save the species from extinction was to undertake a program of captive-breeding to increase its numbers. A number of Condors were captured and divided into two groups, which were placed at the San Diego Zoo and the Los

Angeles Zoo for captive breeding. In 1987, there were only 9 birds left in the wild, and the US government decided to capture them, removing the species completely from the wild, and add all of the remaining birds to the captive breeding program. There were exactly 22 California Condors left in the world.

Over time, a workable method was developed to captive-breed the birds. Normally, Condor pairs only produce one egg per year. But Zoo researchers found that if they removed the egg shortly after it was laid, the female would respond by laying another egg, known as "double-clutching". Researchers were able to coax some birds into laying as many as four eggs per year. These were artificially incubated. To prevent the hatchlings from becoming imprinted on people, they were never allowed to see a human, but were raised using anatomically exact hand puppets that resembled Condor parents.

By 1990, there were enough Condors in captivity to begin planning for a reintroduction back to the wild. In 1991 and 1992, captive-bred Condors were successfully released in California. This success led to the establishment of another captive breeding center in Arizona, and in 1996 captive-bred Condors were reintroduced into the area around the Grand Canyon and in Baja, Mexico. By 2020, the population of California Condors had grown from just 22 birds to almost 450, with about 250 of these living in the wild. It has been confirmed that the released birds are successfully hatching chicks in the wild.

Other successful captive-breeding programs are also being carried out at the San Diego Zoo. Captive-bred Arabian Oryx have been released back to the wild in Jordan, Pandas have been released in China, and Przewalski's Horses have been reintroduced into the Ukraine. The Zoo was also the first institution to successfully breed endangered Hawaiian Palila birds and Maui Parrotbills. And the Zoo has successfully captive-bred Koalas and has the largest population outside of Australia.

In 1972, the Zoo expanded by opening a brand new area called the San Diego Wild Animal Park, now known as the San Diego Zoo Safari Park. This was a huge 1800-acre area where wildlife could live and breed in expansive open-air free-range pastures that mimicked natural habitats from Africa, South America and Asia. Located 30 miles from the Zoo, the Safari Park can be visited by tourists who drive through in their cars (and also tour buses) to see the animals in a natural setting. Much of the Zoological Society's captive-breeding takes place in the Safari Park.

By the 1970s, however, the Zoo was losing visitors as new tourist attractions like Sea World and Disneyland began drawing people away, and the *Zoorama* TV show, which had provided the Zoo with national attention, was cancelled. In response, the Zoological Society selected Joan Embery, a college student who worked part-time in the Kiddie Zoo, as a "Goodwill Ambassador". Embery began doing appearances with live animals on local television shows, which led to a booking on Steve Allen's talk show and then, in November 1971, to an appearance on *The Tonight Show* with Johnny Carson. The show drew in 12 million viewers, and Embery began doing regular segments on the show, over 100 in all. With the publicity, the San Diego Zoo was soon receiving three million visitors a year. Since then, the San Diego Zoo is consistently ranked in poll after poll as the Number One Zoo in the country.

COLUMBUS ZOO
Columbus OH

The first Zoo in Columbus OH was, ironically, a failure. In May 1905, the Columbus Zoological Company opened a small exhibit on Beechwold Boulevard. It struggled financially for five months before closing down. Today, the remains of its front gate and Monkey House can still be seen.

In 1927, another private company opened the Columbus Zoological Gardens in Franklin Park. This Zoo also struggled, but survived long enough to be taken over by the City of Columbus in 1951 and relocated to its present site. In 1970, the Columbus Zoo was turned over to the nonprofit Zoological Park Association. It continued on as a typical mid-sized city Zoo.

Things changed drastically in 1978, when the Zoo began looking for a new director. The person they chose was Jack Hanna, who was at the time directing the tiny Central Florida Zoo near Orlando. A charismatic man with infectious enthusiasm, Hanna convinced the City to fund a complete overhaul of the Zoo, including a program to replace all of the old iron-bar cages with modern open-air enclosures, to build a new Reptile House, and to add a Children's Zoo. Hanna also began a series of fundraising efforts, not only to raise money for these projects, but to increase awareness of the Zoo and to recruit public support for it. As a result, the city's residents voted five separate times to raise their own property taxes to help pay for the Zoo.

To further raise the Zoo's public profile, the telegenic Hanna started a show on local public television featuring the Columbus Zoo and its animals. This in turn led to national TV appearances with David Letterman, Maury Povich, Larry King, and the Good Morning America show.

The Zoo grew steadily, both in size and reputation. By 1986, the nonprofit which ran the Zoo no longer needed any city funding. Between 1978 and 1992, visitors skyrocketed from 350,000 a year to over 1.4 million. The Columbus Zoo was now consistently ranked as one of the top Zoos in the country. A friendly rivalry grew between the Columbus and San Diego Zoos: most years, San Diego took the Number One rating, so when Columbus finally managed to capture the top spot, it ran TV commercials featuring Zookeepers joyously throwing away their shovels and shouting "No more Number Two!" Hanna retired as Director in 1993, but remained as Director Emeritus and continued as the public face of the Zoo in TV shows and press events.

The Columbus Zoo divides its exhibits into zones that are based on geographical and ecological areas, with displays featuring individual species that can be found together in the wild. In 2004, voters passed a resolution allocating $180 million to expand the Zoo by over 100 acres and to add a series of new habitats.

The oldest of these zones is the North American region, which contains much of the original Zoo grounds. It features animals from the US and Canada, especially Ohio natives, and contains Prairie Dogs, Cougars, Bison, Elk, Wolves, Bald Eagles, Moose and Pronghorns. In May 2010, the Polar Frontier exhibit was added to the North America section. This features animals from the Arctic portions of the continent, including Polar Bears, Brown Bears, and Arctic Foxes.

In 2000, the Zoo opened its Congo Expedition area featuring species from Africa. The major attractions here are the Lowland Gorillas. The Columbus Zoo was the first to successfully breed Lowland Gorillas, when "Colo" was born in 1956. She continued to live at the Zoo until her death in 2017 at age 60, making her the oldest Gorilla in captivity. Today, almost half of the Zoo's Gorilla colony are descendants of Colo, and the Zoo's breeding program has produced over 30 offspring. There is also a colony of rare Bonobos, or Pygmy Chimpanzees, on display, along with Leopards, Colobus Monkeys, and Okapis.

The Islands of Southeast Asia exhibit opened in 2003, and was intended to have displays that are more open and immersive. This area features Gibbons and Orangutans. The Asia Quest area was added in 2006. Some of the animals here include Amur Tiger, Red Panda, Sloth Bear, Musk Deer, and Indian Elephant. At one time, the Zoo exhibited a 24-foot Reticulated Python who was the Guinness World Record holder for longest snake in captivity.

Portions of the Walkabout zone opened in 2003 and 2004, centering on species from Australia. The Roadhouse exhibits nocturnal animals like Loris, Kiwi, Binturong, Wombat, and many lizards, while the surrounding area has a walk-through Kangaroo habitat in addition to an exhibit featuring Tasmanian Devils and an aviary with Cockatoos and Lorikeets.

The Shores zone is divided into two sections. The Manatee Coast features species that are native to Florida, and includes Sea Turtles, Pelicans and Stingrays. The Columbus Zoo is one of only two outside of Florida to exhibit Manatees, and it also has a fully-equipped Manatee Hospital for treating rescued animals. The other section here is Discovery Reef, which is centered on an 88,000-gallon Aquarium with tropical fish. There are also seahorses and sharks on display. The Reptile Habitat is also found nearby, which exhibits a large number of snakes, lizards, turtles and frogs.

The largest addition to the Zoo is the Heart of Africa, begun in 2014, which duplicates a portion of the East African plains. The large outdoors enclosure exhibits Zebra, Kudu, Ostrich, Giraffe, Wildebeest and Warthogs, while separate enclosures have African Lions, Hyenas, and Cheetahs.

The newest expansion for the Zoo was the addition of Adventure Cove in 2020. This is intended as an educational area with hands-on experiences. There is a colony of California Sea Lions, and a touch tank of Stingrays.

The Zoo has also added other features to attract a wider audience. In 2000, a restored 1914 carousel, originally built for the now-defunct Olentangy Park, was placed in the Zoo and reopened. A major expansion came in 2008 when the Zoo purchased the land at nearby Wyandot Lake and constructed a water park called "Zoombezi Bay". Plans called for a resort hotel to be built nearby for visitors.

As a result of its expansion, the Columbus Zoo has become one of the most visited Zoos in the world, and it has turned its enormous resources into an extensive network of conservation and education efforts. Over the years the Zoo has contributed financial aid, resources, and technical know-how to a variety of wildlife programs around the world, supporting over 75 projects in almost 40 different countries. These include international efforts such as the Dian Fossey Gorilla Fund and the International Elephant Foundation, as well as local organizations like the Ohio Wildlife Center.

One of the Zoo's most effective conservation efforts has centered on the Mexican wolf, which is now extinct in the wild and has become the subject of an intense captive-breeding effort.

The Gray Wolf, *Canis lupus*, once ranged over most of North America. Once settlers began to flood across the New World, however, farmers and ranchers viewed the Wolf as not only a threat to their livestock but to themselves, and they undertook a systematic campaign to exterminate the predators. Wolves were shot, trapped, and poisoned, and the Federal Government offered a bounty for them. By the middle of the century, they were virtually wiped out, surviving only as scattered packs of stragglers in the emptiest of areas.

In 1929, two biologists named Edward Nelson and Edward Goldman determined that the population of wolves from the American Southwest and Northern Mexico were a distinct subspecies, marked by their narrow skulls, darker color, and smaller size. This was later confirmed by genetic studies. Today the subspecies is recognized as the Mexican Wolf, *Canis lupus baileyi*.

By the time the Mexican subspecies was identified, it was already severely endangered. The primary prey animal for the Mexican Wolf packs was the Cous White-Tail Deer, which in this dry desert area could only survive in the scattered oak/pineland forests. As these disappeared, the Wolves also declined—and this was exacerbated by the methodical human campaign to exterminate them. By 1915 Wolves were rarely encountered anywhere in the US. The last Mexican Wolves seen in New Mexico were in 1927, and by 1970 they had also apparently gone extinct in Texas. Once they were gone in the United States, officials began shipping poisoned bait to Mexican ranchers as a way of wiping the Wolves out there too and preventing them from repopulating the American southwest.

By the 1960s, though, the environmentalist movement began to oppose the slaughter of Wolves. When the Endangered Species Act was passed in 1976 and the Mexican Wolf was listed as "endangered", a thorough survey was done throughout its former range—which turned up only five wild Mexican Wolves, made up of four males and a pregnant female in northern Mexico. Combined with those few that were living in Zoos, that was all that remained of the subspecies.

The US Fish and Wildlife Service formed a Mexican Wolf Recovery Team, which took charge of the effort to re-establish the species through captive breeding. By 1999 there were 179 Mexican Wolves in the breeding program, and the first of these were released into the wild in Arizona and New Mexico. By 2019, there were around 170 wild Mexican Wolves living in the United States and another 40 or so in Mexico. During that same time period, however, around 100 released wolves died in the wild, many due to humans.

In 1992, the Columbus Zoo received a small pack of Mexican Wolves from the Wolf Conservation Center in New York, as part of the Species Survival Plan. Since then, the Zoo has successfully produced 39 pups. At adulthood, one of these pups was then successfully released into the wild in New Mexico, as part of a new pack.

The Mexican Wolf still faces an uphill battle. The extremely low founding population means that even with detailed captive breeding plans, their genome is very limited. They also still encounter open hostility from humans: many people remain opposed to releasing these "dangerous animals", and despite their legal protections, a number of Wolves are killed by ranchers or hunters each year.

SMITHSONIAN NATIONAL ZOO
Washington DC

In 1829, a British chemist and minerologist named James Smithson, a member of the Royal Society of London, died while in Genoa, Italy. The illegitimate son of the Lord of Northumberland and a wealthy widow, Smithson used his family fortune to travel around Europe, writing a total of 27 scientific papers on topics ranging from marine fossils to the chemistry of snake venom.

When he died, he had no children or heirs, so he left an unusual provision in his will: "I then bequeath the whole of my property . . . to the United States of America, to found at Washington, under the name of the Smithsonian Institution, an Establishment for the increase and diffusion of knowledge among men."

To this day, no one knows why Smithson decided to give his fortune to found a scientific institute in a then-obscure country that he had never visited. The British courts, after determining that there were no heirs or other claimants to the fortune, informed US President Andrew Jackson of the bequest in 1835, and in July 1836 Congress voted to accept it and use it to establish the Smithsonian Institution. Smithson's fortune arrived in the US in 1838, in the form of eleven boxes full of British gold coins. These were melted down and minted into American money, worth, in total, $562,483.84—an amount that was almost one-sixtieth of the entire US Government budget at the time. In 1847, construction was begun on the National Mall for the Smithsonian Building. Built of red sandstone, it is now known as the Smithsonian Castle, and it housed the US National Museum. Over the years, the Smithsonian would expand to 19 separate museums, including the Air and Space Museum, the Natural History Museum, and the American History Museum. Today the Smithsonian is one of the leading scientific organizations in the world.

After its establishment as the US National Museum in 1848, the Smithsonian began recruiting scientists and researchers. One of these was William Temple Hornaday, a taxidermist from New York who had caught the Smithsonian's attention with a display of mounted Orangutans in a naturalistic jungle setting. In 1882, Hornaday was hired as a taxidermist for the Smithsonian's Department of Living Animals.

At that time, the taxidermists were keeping a number of live animals for use as models to produce lifelike taxidermy displays, and Hornaday was soon placed in charge of caring for the animals. In 1886, Hornaday's collection of live American Bison, Eagles, Badgers, and a Black Bear was housed in a series of sheds behind the Smithsonian Castle, on the National Mall. Although not intended as an exhibit, the animal display soon proved to be popular with the public, and Hornaday suggested that they be placed in a Smithsonian zoological park for exhibit. In 1889, Congress passed a resolution creating the National Zoo and setting its goals as "the advancement of science and the instruction and recreation of the people." Hornaday had become particularly interested in the conservation of animals such as Bison and Bighorn Sheep that were rapidly disappearing from the American West, and he wanted the new Zoo to be a center for research and conservation as well as education and display.

A Commission was selected, consisting of the US Secretary of the Interior, the Secretary of the Smithsonian, and the

President of the DC Board of Commissioners, to set up the Zoo. An area of 166 acres inside northwest DC, known as Rock Creek, was purchased, and celebrated architect Frederick Law Olmsted designed the landscape and buildings. Hornaday became the first Curator, and the 185 animals being kept by his taxidermists became the core of the National Zoo's collection. This included a number of American Bison, Woodchucks, a Mountain Lion, a Grizzly Bear cub, a Black Bear, a Bald Eagle, several Turkey Vultures, and a collection of turtles and snakes. Soon after, Hornaday conflicted with the Smithsonian Secretary, Samuel Langley, over the direction the Zoo should take, and he left to become head of the New York Zoological Society.

As buildings were constructed, new animals were obtained. In 1891, two Asian Elephants, named "Gold Dust" and "Dunk", were obtained, and shortly later a male African Lion named "French" occupied the Lion House. By 1924, the National Zoo was receiving 2.4 million visitors per year.

During the Depression, workers from the government's Works Progress Administration (WPA) were utilized to construct new buildings, both to house animals and as administrative and support facilities. A number of expeditions went overseas to collect species for the Zoo, including Liberia, Tanganyika, and the Dutch East Indies.

By the 1950's, the National Zoo began to change, becoming closer to Hornaday's original vision of a conservation and research center. The funding system was altered: up until then, half the Zoo's budget had come from the District of Columbia, but now the Zoo would be funded entirely by the Smithsonian, putting it on a more stable footing. The animal-collecting expeditions were ended and a permanent veterinary staff was hired, reflecting a growing emphasis on learning about the needs of captive animals and how to meet them. The Friends Of the National Zoo organization was formed, which gathered supporters in the public, giving the Zoo a base of enthusiastic fans in the community that helped establish and carry out new programs for outreach and education.

In the 1960's, the Zoo formed a "Zoological Research Division" to begin to seriously study the conditions under which Zoo animals were kept, with the goal of learning why some animals did well and others did not, and to determine which Zoo conditions were best to maintain the health of the animals and also encourage breeding. This was partially prompted by the gift in 1964 of two Komodo Dragons from the government of Indonesia. These rare lizards were seriously endangered in the wild, and the National Zoo saw it as its mission to learn how to breed them, both so they could be distributed to other Zoos for display and education, and so captive-bred individuals could be used to supplement the dwindling population in the wild.

To help carry out its new role as a wildlife research and captive breeding center, the Zoo purchased 3200 acres in nearby Virginia, closed to the public, which it called the Conservation and Research Center, later renamed the Smithsonian Conservation Biology Institute. Here, free-roaming populations of endangered species like the Maned Wolf, Przewalski's Horse, and the Scimitar-Horned Oryx were established, and programs begun to captive-breed them. With funding from the Friends Of the National Zoo group, research stations were also established in wild areas around the world to do field biology and scientific research, and to study the environmental needs of both wild and captive animals. The Zoo's veterinary center also trained almost 2000 people from 80 countries as veterinarians and animal technicians, who then went on to train new people in their home countries.

The Zoo's most famous project began in 1972, when US President Richard Nixon re-established American relations with China and visited Beijing. As a goodwill gesture, the Chinese Government donated two Giant Pandas, named Hsing-Hsing and Ling-Ling, to the National Zoo.

Although Pandas, with their distinctive black and white colors, are instantly recognizable to any child who has had stuffed teddy bears, not very much is known about their biology or their lifestyles. They are found only in mountain forests in central China, where their rarity makes it difficult to study them. For some time, there was even a scientific dispute over what group of animals they belonged to: today we know from DNA sequencing that they are bears which have become adapted to a totally vegetarian lifestyle, feeding almost exclusively on bamboo. Because bamboo is so low in nutritional value, the Pandas spend most of their time foraging, eating as much as 40 pounds of bamboo a day. Adult Pandas are about the same size as an American Black Bear, weighing about 250 pounds. The males are a bit bigger than the females.

It is estimated that there are fewer than 2000 Giant Pandas left in the wild, and they are under severe pressure from the rapidly-growing Chinese population, which has been pushing into their habitat and converting the wild bamboo groves to farmland. The danger to wild Panda population is especially great because of their breeding habits. Pandas don't reach breeding age until they are 4-8 years old, and then the female only comes into breeding condition for a short period of just two weeks in the spring (but are only fertile when they are actually ovulating, a period of just two days). A single cub is born three or four months later: it is hairless, blind, and helpless, about the size of a hamster. It will be at least two years before the female is ready to mate again. Because they breed so slowly, it is difficult for Panda populations to rebuild once they have been reduced in number.

When the Smithsonian received Hsing-Hsing and Ling-Ling in 1972, it immediately began laying plans to captive-breed them. This turned out to be far more difficult than imagined. Both Pandas had been taken from the wild at a very young age, and they did not have much experience with other Pandas. In the wild, male Pandas compete with each other to mate with the female during her brief period of receptiveness, and the younger inexperienced males get to watch and learn from the older ones. Hsing-Hsing, however, had never had that experience, and when it came time for mating with Ling-Ling, he didn't know how. At one point, the Zoo staff even resorted to "panda porno", projecting films of mating pandas into their enclosures to show the pair what to do. In the end, it took Hsing-Hsing ten years to figure it out. When he did, Ling-Ling conceived a total of five cubs over the next several years. But now, Ling-Ling's inexperience came into play: she didn't know how to care for the cubs, and none of them lived past infancy.

To try to save the species, China has now placed most of the Panda's habitat area into a national park, and has set up its own captive-breeding program at the Chengdu Research Base. It has also sent a number of breeding pairs out to Zoos all over the world, including Asia, Australia, Europe and seven Zoos in the US, Canada and Mexico. In all, there are about 300 Pandas on loan to captive-breeding programs worldwide. Typically, the loan agreement is for a term of ten years, and the host Zoo pays as much as $1 million a year to the Chinese wildlife program. In addition, the Zoo has to meet the costs of maintaining the Pandas (which is about five times more expensive than maintaining Elephants, making Pandas by far the most expensive animals to keep in captivity). Under the loan agreement, any offspring from the Pandas belong to China, and can be returned to the wild to expand the populations there.

Sadly, things have not worked out well. Although knowledge has improved in the decades since Hsing-Hsing and Ling-Ling and dozens of Pandas have now been born in captivity (many of them in North America), only a handful of captive-bred offspring have been reintroduced to the wild— and one of those was killed by other wild Pandas. China plans on releasing just one captive-bred Panda per year until more is learned about how to successfully reintroduce them.

As a result of this limited success, the entire Panda breeding program has become the subject of debate within the wildlife conservation community. Because Pandas are cuddly and cute, they receive a massive amount of support from the public, with Panda conservation programs routinely receiving millions of dollars per year from public contributions. Yet despite all that funding, the results have been disappointing, and many are now arguing that the money could be more effectively put to use protecting other species and especially in preserving habitat. Others have responded that the Panda has become an icon of the entire conservation movement, and it is important as a symbol to keep people engaged and interested so they continue to support *all* conservation efforts, both financially and politically.

At the Smithsonian, the staff at the National Zoo remains committed to Panda captive-breeding. After Hsing-Hsing and Ling-Ling died in the 1990's, the National Zoo received two more Pandas on loan, named Mei Xiang and Tian Tian. By

2018 they had four cubs. The first, Tai Shan, was born in 2005 and was returned to China in 2010, where he is now part of China's breeding program. In September 2012, after being artificially inseminated, Mei Xiang gave birth to a female cub that died shortly later. And in August 2013, after another artificial insemination, twin cubs were born: one died at birth, the other, named Bao Bao, was returned to China in 2017.

The Zoo also had success with its Komodo Dragon breeding program, and has now sent pairs of its adult offspring to several other Zoos in the US for further breeding.

In the early 2000's, the National Zoo came under heavy criticism, after a number of animals died from illness and accidents. The AZA dropped the Zoo's accreditation to "provisional", and a committee from the American Academy of Sciences was assigned to evaluate the Zoo's practices. The Zoo director resigned after it was discovered that some veterinary records had been altered.

During this time, the Zoo continued to expand and opened a number of new exhibits. In 1992, the Amazonia exhibit opened, featuring a large collection of South American plants, fish, invertebrates and wildlife displayed in naturalistic settings. The Kids Farm exhibit, with Goats, Sheep and Cows, opened in 2004, and the Asia Trail opened in 2006.

As of the early 2020s, the National Zoo has 1800 animals on exhibit from 300 species (about one-fourth of which are endangered). As a part of the Smithsonian Institution the Zoo has free admission, and it receives about 2 million visitors per year.

BRONX ZOO
New York, NY

Theodore Roosevelt was a man larger than life. He commanded the famous Rough Riders regiment in the Spanish-American War, he served as Governor of New York, and as US Vice President and President. He was also an avid adventurer and big-game hunter who made expeditions to South America and Africa, and a conservationist who helped establish the very first National Parks.

In 1887, Roosevelt was one of the founding members of the Boone and Crockett Club, made up mostly of wealthy and influential northeasterners with an interest in big-game hunting and nature. Their goal was to protect the rapidly-shrinking wilderness areas of the American West.

As part of this program, the Club advocated the establishment of zoological parks as a way of educating the public, and in 1895 Club members in New York City, led by Madison Grant and C. Grant LaFarge, formed the New York Zoological Society to raise money for a Zoo. New York was already one of the largest cities in the world with a number of noted museums and parks, and the Society felt that it was lacking only a world-class Zoo. They set out to build one.

The first step was to choose a location. The Society's charter specified that the Zoo had to be located within the city limits, and they also wanted an area that would be easily accessible to as many people as possible. Eventually they settled on a 250-acre tract of land along the Bronx River, next to the planned Botanical Garden. It was sold to the city by Fordham University for just $1,000 specifically for the Zoo.

The next step was to design the new exhibits. While most Zoos at this time were still using old-fashioned iron-bar cells, the Zoological Society wanted something more modern, and settled on open-air enclosures instead. In asking the City for help with funding, the Society described its planned Zoo as "a zoological park in which the larger and more important native animals have free range in large inclosures, where a satisfactory attempt can be made to copy or suggest natural haunts, and where visitors can find enjoyment in the contemplation of fine, healthy animals amid beautiful natural surroundings." The Zoo's layout was designed by local architects Heins & LaFarge, who placed a number of buildings to surround the central "Astor Court".

The Bronx Zoo opened in November 1899, with 22 exhibit areas and 843 animals. William Temple Hornaday, who had already served at the Smithsonian Zoo in Washington DC, was hired on as Director. He had a particular interest in American Bison, which once covered the American Plains but which were now already in serious decline. With the help of Teddy Roosevelt, Hornaday formed the American Bison Society and set up a captive-breeding program at the Zoo. By 1907, captive-bred Bison from the Bronx Zoo were being released into the wild in several western National Parks to re-establish herds. Today the Zoo still has its own herd on exhibit in the Bison Range area.

Under Hornaday's leadership, the Zoo continued to expand. He obtained several Thylacines, or Marsupial Wolves, from Tasmania—making the Bronx Zoo one of only two Zoos in the United States to exhibit these animals. Unfortunately, the Thylacines arrived in poor health and proved difficult to keep in captivity, and despite desperate attempts to breed them, they were all dead by 1919. The species itself went extinct not long after, with the last one dying in an Australian zoo in 1936. Hornaday also made attempts to breed Barbary Lions, a distinct subspecies from North Africa which was also dwindling in the wild, but this failed too, and this subspecies also became extinct.

In 1906, however, Hornaday sparked a storm of controversy.

In 1904, the city of St Louis had been selected to host that year's World Fair. A number of people were dispatched to gather up some natives to display, along with their traditional housing and cultural items. Members of several different Native American tribes were brought to St Louis, including the famed Apache war leader Geronimo, released from his military prison by a special order from the Secretary of War. Groups of Inuit "Eskimos" were also brought in from Alaska, as well as natives from the recently-conquered Hawaii, Samoa, and Philippine Islands. There were native Patagonians from South America, and Ainu from northern Japan. And from Africa came a member of the Mbuti tribe in the Belgian Congo, named Ota Benga. It was, in essence, a human zoo.

When the World's Fair closed down after almost a year, Ota Benga ended up at the American Museum of Natural History in New York City, which agreed to let the African live in a spare room inside the museum. Things did not go well—he who spoke no English and felt isolated and alone, and grew increasingly sullen and hostile. The Museum then contacted Hornaday at the Bronx Zoo. Ota Benga was given a place to sleep in a spare room and was given free run of the Zoo, and began spending several hours a day in the Monkey House.

The Zoo visitors, in turn, were intrigued by the sight of an African "pigmy" interacting with the apes, and Hornaday realized that he had a potential crowd-draw on his hands. He encouraged Ota Benga to spend more time in the Monkey House. Over several weeks, the African was given a set of bow and arrows and spent some time each day shooting at a target. Parrots were added to the Monkey House to give it more of a "jungle" flavor, and several bones were scattered around the floor (including, it was reported, some human bones, to give a tantalizing hint of cannibalism).

The visitors were delighted. So was Hornaday. One weekend a new sign appeared in the Monkey House: "The African Pigmy, 'Ota Benga.' Age, 23 years. Height, 4 feet 11 inches. Weight, 103 pounds. Brought from the Kasai River,

Congo Free State, South Central Africa, by Dr. Samuel P. Verner. Exhibited each afternoon during September." Visitorship soared to 40,000 per day as curious New Yorkers lined up to see the unusual spectacle.

But the "man in the Zoo" sparked immediate outrage and controversy, led mostly by the local New York African-American community. Within two weeks the offending sign was taken down, Ota Benga was banned from the Monkey House, and was sent to a foster family in Lynchburg VA, where his filed-down teeth were capped, he went to a Baptist school to learn English, and he changed his name to "Otto Bingo". He got a job working in a tobacco warehouse.

By this time, however, "Otto Bingo" had seen enough of American society, and what he wanted most was to go home to the Congo. But in 1914, the First World War broke out, and passenger ship traffic between North America and Africa came to a halt. As the war dragged on, it must have seemed to him that he would never be able to return home. In March 1916, Ota Binga walked into a patch of woods, chipped the caps off his teeth with a rock, made a ceremonial fire, and shot himself with a stolen pistol.

The whole sorry incident remains as one of the most tragic episodes in zoo history.

The Bronx Zoo is consistently ranked as one of the top Zoological parks in the country. Among the Zoo's exhibit areas are the African Plains, Himalayan Highlands, Mouse House, Madagascar, Jungle World, World of Birds, Congo Gorilla Forest, and Mitsubishi Riverwalk. There are 650 species on exhibit, and the Zoological society (now renamed the Wildlife Conservation Society) sponsors scientific research all around the world. When the cash-strapped City of New York severely cut its funding for the Zoo in the 2010s, the Conservation Society continued its work using donations and contributions. In addition to the Bronx Zoo, the WCS also manages the Central Park Zoo, Prospect Park Zoo, Queens Zoo, and the New York Aquarium.

One of the Society's most successful conservation programs is being done with the Snow Leopard, as part of the Species Survival Plan.

The Snow Leopard (*Panthera uncia*) is found in the mountain ranges that run from Pakistan up to southern Siberia and across to China, especially the Himalayan, Pamir, and Altai Mountains. The cat was first scientifically described in 1777 based on a skin, and as more samples arrived in Europe these were attributed to a number of different species and subspecies, but modern study shows that all of the various populations are the same species and interbreed with each other often enough to maintain a single gene pool. Genetic studies show that the Snow Leopard is closely related to the other Asian leopards and has hybridized with them in the past.

Weighing around 100 pounds, this large cat is adapted to a harsh environment where few other animals can survive. The thick pelt protects from the cold, while the pattern of dark splotches on light-colored fur provides camouflage on the snowy rocks. The nasal cavity is unusually long and wide, which allows it to warm the thin mountain air before it is drawn into the lungs. Snow Leopards have wide feet that act as snowshoes, and the ears are small to prevent frostbite. The long tail serves as a balancing rod when the cat moves along rocky ridges, and also acts as a reservoir to store body fat for lean periods. The Leopards often wrap their furry tail across their face while they sleep.

In the wild, Snow Leopards can live up to 15 years. They reach breeding size at two years old, when they wander in search of a mate. Mating takes place in the winter and 2-3 cubs are born in spring.

Although they are capable of hunting in deep snow, the Leopards spend most of their time in the forested regions on the lower mountain slopes, sometimes crossing ice fields from one mountain to another. Here they hunt a variety of prey ranging from Deer and wild Goats to Marmots and Pika, and have also been known to kill Langurs and Red Pandas. Each solitary cat patrols its own hunting area, though mated pairs have sometimes been reported as hunting together.

In some areas, Snow Leopards are blamed for killing domestic livestock, and villagers often make attempts to drive the predators away. The cats are shy and retiring, and prefer to inhabit areas where there are no humans. This has led to a loss of habitat as human habitation grows, and Snow Leopards are now severely endangered in the wild. The issue has been exacerbated by poaching and illegal hunting for the highly-prized thick fur, which is used for luxury coats. Studies have also predicted that global warming will reduce the cat's mountain habitat by as much as one-third. It is estimated that there are less than 7,000 wild Snow Leopards remaining throughout their range.

In 2013, all twelve of the nations in which wild Snow Leopard populations can be found gathered together in the Global Snow Leopard Forum and made conservation plans that became integrated into the Global Snow Leopard and Ecosystem Protection Program (GSLEP). GSLEP spells out steps to protect Leopard habitat within National Parks and to captive-breed them for release, with the goal of establishing at least twenty new self-sustaining wild populations throughout their range. The program is supported by a variety of nonprofit institutions, and much of this effort centers on the 600 or so Snow Leopards being kept in Zoos around the world, which became the focus of captive breeding.

The Bronx Zoo, which was one of the first Zoos in the US to exhibit Snow Leopards back in 1903, has been at the forefront of this effort. In August 2006, a goatherder in Pakistan's Naltar Valley found two orphaned Snow Leopard cubs whose mother had been killed in a landslide. He tried to keep them as pets, but when one of them died, he turned the remaining cub, a male, over to authorities. Since there were no Snow Leopard rescue centers in Pakistan, the cub, dubbed "Leo", was sent to the Bronx Zoo, with the understanding that the Conservation Society would help Pakistan establish its own Snow Leopard program.

In 2013, Leo was joined by other Leopards and became part of the captive breeding arrangement, and in April the Zoo had their first cub, named Naltar. Since that time, the Zoo's program has produced over 70 Snow Leopard cubs, which have all been integrated into the international Species Survival Plan and have been distributed to other Zoos to produce the maximum genetic diversity.

BUSCH GARDENS
Tampa FL

Busch Gardens is a hybrid—half amusement park, half Zoo. Once owned by the Annheuser-Busch beer company, it was sold years ago to a holding corporation when A-B was bought by the Belgian beer conglomerate InBev. There are two Busch Gardens in the US—the one in Williamsburg VA has a European theme, and the one in Tampa Bay has an African theme.

In 1905, one of the wealthiest men in St Louis was Adolphus Busch, co-owner of the Annheuser-Busch beer company. In addition to beer, Adolphus had two other passions—birds and flowers. And so at his winter home in Pasadena, California, Busch and his wife Lily built an immense outdoors garden, with tropical plants from all over the world. The garden also included an enclosed aviary with exotic parrots.

By 1906, so many people were asking to see Busch's garden that he decided to open it to the public. In 1909, after Lily Busch installed a number of statues depicting fairytale stories, the "Lower Garden" was also opened for viewing. Extending over about 30 acres, "Busch's Garden" became a popular tourist destination, and was even given its own station along the Pacific Railway.

When Adolphus died in 1913, Lily offered to donate the entire garden to Pasadena as a public park, but the city declined. For the next 25 years, the garden remained open to the public, and was also utilized by nearby Hollywood film studios as a filming location. Among the motion pictures that had scenes shot at Busch Garden were "Gone With the Wind", "Frankenstein", and "The Adventures of Robin Hood". In 1938, the garden was closed down, subdivided, and sold off.

But when the Annheuser-Busch Company opened a new brewery in Van Nuys, California, in 1954, the Busch family remembered the Pasadena garden, and decided to resurrect the idea and use it to promote their beer. A new "Busch Gardens" was opened next door to the brewery, which featured 17 acres of tropical plants and a parrot aviary. There were boat rides on the lake, a trolley loop around the park, and a futuristic monorail. Visitors were also invited to try free samples of Annheuser-Busch beer and tours were offered of the nearby brewery.

In December 1976, with the number of visitors dwindling, the Van Nuys garden was closed. But the company had already begun a much more extensive, and ultimately more successful, project. In 1959, another "Busch Gardens" was opened next door to the brewery in Tampa, Florida. Originally, visitors to the tropical garden were taken care of by four employees and four parrots. But the facility was quickly expanded to include a hospitality house for free beer samples, a much larger aviary, boat rides, and a luxury restaurant known as "The Old Swiss House". In 1965, it was decided to expand the animal collection and to focus on an "Africa" theme. The Park became known as "Busch Gardens The Dark Continent", and a large open 70-acre area was set up as an "African Plains" exhibit, with a monorail and a train ride (the "Serengeti Express", which still operates today) for viewing the animals. It was, at the time, an entirely new concept for a Zoo, and the advertising proudly proclaimed it the place "where the people are caged and the animals roam free". Busch Gardens Tampa became enormously popular, and by 1968 it was the most-visited attraction in Florida, with 3 million tourists a year.

Meanwhile, another theme park had been opened in Van Nuys CA in 1966, which included boat rides, a monorail and a bird sanctuary. It never gained a large following, however, and closed ten years later.

In 1971, Walt Disney World resort debuted in Orlando, Florida. Although Busch Gardens Tampa had always been viewed by the beer company as a promotional gimmick and a private hobby for the Busch family (who had an interest in wildlife and in animal rescue), it was now decided to add some exciting thrill rides to the theme park to allow it to continue to attract enough visitors to be self-sustaining. The park's first roller-coaster, "Scorpion", opened in 1976. New rides continued to be added until Busch Gardens Tampa was one of the largest amusement parks, as well as one of the largest Zoos, in the US.

Two new parks were also opened. In 1971, Busch Gardens Houston followed the same "zoo/amusement park" formula as Busch Gardens Tampa, but with an "Asia" theme. It struggled for a short time before closing in 1973. Busch Gardens Williamsburg, originally named "The Old Country", was more successful. It opened in Virginia in 1975 with a "European" theme, and functioned mostly as an amusement park.

The Annheuser-Busch Company also owned the very popular Sea World parks which appeared in San Diego, Orlando, and San Antonio. In 2008, there were plans in the works to open another Busch Gardens, accompanied by a Sea World, in the resort city of Dubai in the United Arab Emirates. That plan fell through when the Great Recession crippled the financing.

By this time, the beer industry, which had long been dominated by American companies, began to change. Global competitors began buying up the American giants: Coors was sold to a Canadian company, and a South African corporation bought Miller. In 2009, the giant InBev brewery, headquartered in Belgium, purchased the Annheuser-Busch Company. InBev did not want to be in the amusement park business, and so Busch Gardens Tampa, Busch Gardens Williamsburg, and all three Sea Worlds were sold off to the Blackstone Group, a Wall Street investment firm. While the

Busch Company had run the parks as promotional assets and as the personal pet projects of the Busch family, the Blackstone Group was running them to make a profit.

In 2017, Blackstone sold its share of the parks to the Zhonghong Zhuoye Group, a Chinese investment company, but just two years later Zhonghong ran into financial difficulties and its share of stock was obtained by the Hill Path Capital company.

Despite all the ups and downs, however, Busch Gardens has always remained a fully functional Zoo as well as a theme park, and like Sea World it participates in education and captive-breeding programs for a number of endangered species. One of these is for the Hawaiian Goose, also known as the Nene.

When the Hawaiian Islands emerged from the sea, one by one as a series of volcanic mountains, they were empty and barren. The only life that could reach them were windborne plant seeds and animals that could fly or raft here on floating mats of vegetation. On the tiny isolated islands, these species adapted to the new environment and evolved into some of the most unique and rare ecosystems in the world.

About half a million years ago, a flock of Canada Geese (*Branta canadensis*) somehow became stranded on the islands. Perhaps they were caught in a storm and blown off course. But compared to their ancestral Canadian home, the islands, which included the newly-emerged "big island" of Hawaii, were a tropical paradise, with abundant food and few predators. Over time, the introduced Canada Goose population thrived, and as it adapted to its new home it split into two new species. One of these became the much larger (but now extinct) Hawaiian Giant Goose. The other adapted to island life by becoming smaller (a common phenomenon known as "island dwarfism") and is now known as the Hawaiian Goose or Nene (*Branta sandvicensis*).

The Nene looks similar to the Canada Goose, but is noticeably smaller, and has tan-colored check patches and a tan neck. It makes many of the same honking sounds as its Canadian ancestor, but also has a distinctive "nay-nay" call, from which it gets its name. Because its Hawaiian environment had few predators, the Nene has mostly given up flight, and instead has evolved longer legs and feet that are only partly webbed, allowing it to walk and run on the ground.

Like all geese, the Nene is herbivorous, and grazes on grasses, leaves, flowers, and sometimes on soft fruits. However unlike most geese, which are aquatic, the Nene prefers to live inland on the island hills, where it grazes in grasslands and old lava flows. In modern times, they are commonly seen on golf courses.

The Geese breed almost year-round, avoiding only the heat of summer. Nests are made with rocks on bare lava fields, where the female will lay 3-5 eggs while the male watches over her. Since there are few predators to attack them, the females go into a sort of hypnotic trance while incubating the eggs for around 30 days. The newly-hatched goslings are capable of running and feeding themselves, and stay near their parents until the next nesting season.

At one time the Nene inhabited virtually every one of the Hawaiian Islands, with an estimated 25-30,000 individual birds. When Native Hawaiians arrived, they hunted the Geese for food, but seem to have had only a minor impact.

The real trouble began when Europeans arrived. The first of these was the British explorer Captain James Cook in 1778. Not only did the Europeans hunt the Geese relentlessly, but they brought to the islands (intentionally or unintentionally) nonnative predators such as cats, mongooses, rats, and pigs. These attacked the nestlings and eggs of many ground-nesting birds like the Nene, who had all evolved in the absence of ground predators and had no way to defend against the onslaught. Bird populations declined and the islands became depopulated. The Nene was hard hit. By 1890, there were only remnant populations left on the larger islands. In 1949, researchers were only able to find 30 individual Geese remaining.

Because the Nene is the State Bird of Hawaii, officials took a special interest in preserving the species, and in 1967 the bird was listed on the Federal Endangered Species Act, while protected habitat areas were established at Volcanoes National Park, Haleakala National Park, and the Maui Bird Conservation Center. All of the remaining wild birds were captured, and small flocks were dispersed to Zoos and conservation centers around the world, who began captive-breeding programs to increase their numbers. Over the years, wild populations were re-established in the Kilauea Point and Hakalau Forest National Wildlife Refuges, and in 2003 a program was established on Molokai to encourage private ranchers and landowners to set aside habitat for reintroduced Nene. In 2014 a pair of Nene were established in the James Campbell National Wildlife Refuge on Oahu.

Today there are around 4,000 Nene, with about half of these in the wild. Self-sustaining breeding populations have been established in the wild on the islands of Hawaii, Maui, Molokai and Kauai. Although the Nene is still in danger, these conservation efforts have so far been successful, and it has been downgraded from "endangered" to "threatened" status.

At Busch Gardens, the Nenes are not part of the wild-release program, but are instead part of the "assurance collection". This is an important element of the overall conservation program. With their dwindling numbers and limited geographic range, most endangered species are very vulnerable to a sudden unexpected catastrophe such as a disease outbreak, a drought or flood, or a natural disaster like a hurricane or wildfire. To defend against this possibility, Zoos establish an "assurance collection", which serves as a sort of insurance policy for the species. If some sudden disaster were to wipe out the wild population, the assurance population would still be safe, and could then be used to re-establish the species in the wild. For maximum protection, the assurance collection is spread out over a number of different Zoos.

So, while most of the Nene captive-release program is concentrated in a small number of facilities, the assurance colony is dispersed over a large geographic area, including Busch Gardens. Here they are bred for exhibit in other Zoos, both as a way to increase their numbers and as a way of educating the public about the plight of these rare birds.

DISNEY ANIMAL KINGDOM
Orlando FL

If Busch Gardens Tampa is half-amusement park and half-zoo, Walt Disney World's Animal Kingdom was founded with an even bigger identity problem. It was planned from the beginning as a wildlife-themed amusement park, in which the animals were intended as show props. In all of its early advertising, Disney stressed that Animal Kingdom was "NataZoo". Yet it has one of the largest collections of live animals in Florida.

By the mid-1980s, the Disney theme parks in California and Florida were riding high. Walt Disney World Resort was the number one tourist attraction in the world, and CEO Michael Eisner was making ambitious plans for total domination of the tourist trade in Orlando, by expanding Disney World to such an extent that visitors could spend their entire vacation there without ever having to leave Disney property. The first stage was the addition of "The Living Seas" exhibit to EPCOT. It featured large aquariums with tropical reef fish and sharks and educational displays, but the real purpose of the expansion was purely business-based—it was intended to stop Disney guests from going to Sea World. Next came the Disney-MGM Studios (later renamed as Hollywood Studios), which celebrated the golden era of movies—but whose real purpose was to prevent Disney guests from visiting Universal Studios.

The next target was Busch Gardens Tampa, only 90 minutes away from Disney World. Plans called for an immense new park, almost 600 acres—the largest one Disney had ever built—to be called Disney's Beastly Kingdom. It would consist of three themed sections: one would celebrate animals that exist today, another would focus on animals that existed in the past, and the third would center around nonexistent animals of fantasy and legend. The whole project was budgeted at $750 million.

It soon became apparent, however, that this immense project would be too grand even for Disney's deep pockets, and the concept was scaled down. The "mythical animals" section, which would have featured dragons, unicorns, centaurs and sea monsters, was dropped. The "animals of the past" section was scaled down and was also tied in to one of Disney's upcoming movies about animated dinosaurs, and would feature prehistoric-themed rides. It became Dinoland USA. The rest of the park would focus on "animals of the present", and would include children's favorites like Elephants, Giraffes, and Lions, all of which would be incorporated into story-driven tram and train rides. The park would initially open with its Africa section, which would feature storylines from the planned Disney movie "The Lion King". Later, an Asian-themed section would follow. The new park would be called Animal Kingdom.

Disney went all-out. The center showpiece of the new park was "The Tree of Life", a giant sculptured tree featuring animal carvings that was built around a framework adapted from a giant oil rig. Inside the Tree of Life was an entire theater devoted to a 4d show based on the Disney movie "A Bug's Life". A complete replica East African village named Harambe was built, with shops, restaurants, a bar, and African performers and musicians.

Animal Kingdom opened in April 1998, with the Asian "Expedition Everest" section following in 2008. Its rollercoaster ride featured a giant animatronic Yeti, a harkening back to the original "animals of fantasy" idea. In 2019 Disney negotiated a deal with 20th Century Fox and opened a new section based on the sci-fi creatures from the James Cameron film "Avatar". "The World of Pandora" replaced Camp Minnie Mickey, which was itself just a temporary replacement for the earlier cancelled fantasy section.

Most of the live animals at Animal Kingdom are inside the "Africa" and "Asia" sections. The basic idea was to build rides with an ecological and conservation theme, but to use live animals instead of animatronics. This required careful planning to insure that the animals would always be in view of the guests at the proper times, unobstructed by fences or walls. At the same time, the animals themselves had to be properly kept and cared for. It was a major undertaking and something Disney's "Imagineers" had never attempted before, so they consulted extensively with experts from the Bronx and San Diego Zoos to learn how to set up enclosures that would serve both animal-care and story-telling needs. The open-air paddocks use cleverly-hidden ditches and moats to keep the animals confined, and also utilize hidden feeding stations, heated or cooled rocks, and other tricks to entice the animals to stay out in the open where they can be easily seen by visitors.

In the Africa section, live animals are featured in two rides and one walking trail. In Kilimanjaro Safaris, visitors ride in open-sided trams through a carefully-arranged series of enclosures depicting African savannah wildlife. There are Lions, Cheetahs, Elephants, Rhinos, Ostriches, and Antelopes. Originally there was an audio narration accompanying the ride which told a story involving a narrow escape from Elephant poachers, but Disney decided that this was too upsetting for the little kids and dropped it. In Rafiki's Planet Watch, a small train takes guests to a "Lion King" themed display of animals and educational exhibits, including a look inside the veterinary hospital. In Gorilla Falls Exploration Trail, a walking path leads to enclosures with Gorillas, Colobus Monkeys, Okapi and an aviary. In the Asia section of the park, the Maharajah Jungle Trek is a walkway which passes enclosures containing Bengal Tigers, Komodo Dragons, Gibbons, Fruit Bats and another aviary. As with the World Showcase area of EPCOT, all of the Disney staff in the African and Asian sections are actually residents of the region that is represented.

Although Disney Animal Kingdom was designed and arranged as a theme park, the sheer number of animals here means that the facility has to operate as a Zoo, too—whether it wants to or not. Disney faces all the same challenges as any other Zoo its size, and it meets them in the same way. There is an extensive staff of zookeepers and veterinarians, and the park is fully AZA certified and meets all the mandated requirements for animal care and safety.

Animal Kingdom also participates in conservation and breeding programs for many of the species that it keeps. The park has bred Giraffes, Elephants and White Rhinos. Most of these are part of assurance colonies, but several of the captive-bred White Rhinos were later reintroduced to the wild in a national park in Uganda.

The White Rhino (*Ceratotherium simum*) is differentiated from the rarer Black Rhino (*Diceros bicornis*) by its snout: the White Rhino is a plains grazer and has wide square lips for nipping off grass, while the Black Rhino is a forest browser and has narrow pointed lips for plucking leaves from trees.

There are two different subspecies of White Rhino in Africa. The Northern White Rhino was formerly found from Chad and Sudan down to Uganda, but has now been exterminated from the wild. As of the early 2020s, only two Northern White Rhinos still survive. Both are in a wildlife preserve in Kenya, and both are females (the last male Northern White Rhino died in a Zoo in 2018). The only remaining hope for the subspecies is the use of sperm, taken from the last males before they died and frozen to preserve it, to artificially inseminate eggs from the two remaining females. In 2019 three viable embryos were successfully created *in vitro*: they were frozen and are now awaiting experiments with a suitable surrogate mother.

The Southern White Rhino subspecies historically ranged from South Africa up to Uganda. By the 1890s they were almost extinct, with the last known population, on Zulu land in South Africa, numbering less than 100. After being granted legal protection, they have recovered somewhat, and captive-bred White Rhinos have been re-introduced in Zimbabwe,

Botswana, Uganda and Namibia. It is now estimated that there are about 20,000 Southern White Rhinos in the wild, most in Kenya and South Africa. This represents a near doubling of the population since the 1990s, but the species is still listed as "threatened".

For half a century, Rhinos have been the poster animals for endangered species. "Traditional Asian medicine" has long held that powdered Rhino horn is not only a cure for all sorts of various diseases and ailments, from fever to vomiting to headache to joint pain, but is also a powerful aphrodisiac that will cure male impotence. This is all, of course, simply nonsense—Rhino horn contains no bone, but is made from compressed hair composed of the protein keratin, the same material which makes up human hair and nails. So powdered Rhino horn is no different than fingernail clippings. It does not treat or cure anything at all.

By the 1970s, all of the world's Rhino species were on the verge of extinction, with poaching one of the primary causes. Some of this demand was centered in the oil-rich Middle East, where Rhino horn was traditionally used for the handles of ceremonial daggers carried by desert tribesmen. But most poached Rhino horn went to Asia for "medicine". Nations in eastern and southern Africa made tremendous efforts to combat poachers and protect their remaining Rhino herds, with some measure of success. In some areas, the Rhino populations began to slowly recover.

But by the 1990's, rising wealth in China and India began the process all over again. Poaching once more increased steadily, fueled by the growing demand for "medicinals" in Asia. These poaching rings can be very sophisticated, making use of technology like helicopters, night vision goggles, and silenced high-powered rifles. Some poachers are tracking Rhino herds through GPS-tagged photos taken by unwitting tourists and posted on social media. A few African countries have virtually given up on even attempting to stop the poachers, but even in countries with strict enforcement, the astounding amounts of money that can be made are enough to entice many poor and struggling people to take the risk.

Since the Asian species of Rhino, in Java and Sumatra, are so critically rare that even the poachers have trouble finding them, most of the "traditional medicine" powdered horn in China and India now comes from Africa. When a Vietnamese government official announced in 2006 that powdered Rhino horn had cured his relative of cancer, there was an immediate spike in demand, an immediate increase in price—and over 300 White and Black Rhinos were poached in South Africa alone. Illegally-killed Rhinos are now so insanely valuable on the black market that not even Zoo Rhinos are safe—poachers killed a White Rhino in a Zoo in France in 2017, and Zoos in Africa have had to hire round-the-clock armed guards to protect their Rhinos. And with almost three billion potential customers in China and India, there simply are not enough Rhinos in the entire world to feed the demand. The future of all the world's Rhino species is precarious.

SAN ANTONIO ZOO
San Antonio TX

In the first years of the 1900s, a traveling circus was stranded in San Antonio when it ran out of money, and the owner was forced to quarter his performing animals in fenced pens at San Pedro Park. Here, he began charging local residents to come and look at them. It was San Antonio's first unofficial "Zoo".

In 1914, George W. Brackenridge, the publisher of the local *San Antonio Express-News*, donated a large tract of land to the city which became known as Brackenridge Park. The remaining animals in San Pedro Park were purchased by the city and moved to the new park, where they joined the publisher's own collection of four bears, two lions, and a number of monkeys, deer and buffalo. This tiny "Zoo" opened to the public in March. Over time, a golden eagle, a weasel, and a prairie wolf were added to the collection.

Finally in 1928 a nonprofit San Antonio Zoological Society was established to set up an official zoological park. A 35-acre area of land in Brackenridge and Koehler Parks was selected. This was formerly a limestone quarry, and its flat areas bordered by steep cliffs, along with a stretch of the San Antonio River that flowed through it, made this site ideal for the modern free-range enclosures that were envisioned. The

San Antonio Zoo opened in 1929 with 344 animals on display as well as an outdoors Monkey Island. The first Zoo Director was Fred Stark, who had worked with the earlier bird collections.

Obtaining support from the city and the public, Stark built the Zoo into one of finest in the US. An Aquarium building was added in 1948, and the Zoo was further expanded in 1969 with a Bird House containing a simulated indoors jungle and free-flight aviaries. It grew into the second-largest bird collection in the world. The Zoo also exhibited a large number of hoofed animals. Many of these came from the USDA, which set up a quarantine point for imported ungulates nearby and donated confiscated or abandoned animals to the Zoo. This led to exhibits of exotic and endangered antelopes like Addrea Gazelles, Dama Gazelles, Scimitar-Horned Oryx, and Sable Antelope.

At one point, the Zoo became indirectly involved in one of the oddest hapenings in Texas history.

In 1956, the city decided to add an attraction to Brackenridge Park. The new "choo-choo train ride" featured a one-fifth-scale copy of a General Motors diesel passenger train engine that was running on the Missouri-Pacific railroad. Officially known as the "Brackenridge Eagle" but popularly known as "Old No. 99", the train carried park visitors on a three-mile loop of 12-inch track, and was at the time the longest miniature train ride in the world. It made stops at locations around the park, including the Zoo, the Train Depot Café, the Witte Museum, and the Japanese Tea Garden, and soon became a popular attraction for kids and weekend visitors.

Shortly past noon on Saturday, July 17, 1970, "Old No. 99" was chugging around the park with about 75 weekend passengers. As the miniature locomotive approached a bend in the tracks and slowed down, however, two men sprang out from behind some bushes and ran to the driver, waving guns. As the train stopped, most of the passengers assumed it was a prank or a staged performance—until one of the men leveled his pistol at one of them and shouted, "Lady, this is no joke." While one of the gunmen held the engineer at bay, the other went down the entire train with a couple of pillow cases, systematically collecting wallets, purses, cameras, watches, and jewelry. Once the thieves had robbed everyone, they ran off.

The startled engineer proceeded to the nearest stop and notified the cops. Listening to the police scanner in his office was John Polich, a reporter for the *San Antonio Express and News*. He could not believe his ears: not only had there not been an actual train robbery in the Wild West since the 1920s, but the city park's choo-choo train ride was just about the strangest target for a robbery that he could think of. Polich went to the scene and interviewed many of the robbery victims, and his front page story ran the next day and was picked up all over the state. It was dubbed the "Great (Little) Train Robbery."

After a time, the two thieves were caught (they turned out to be US Army soldiers from nearby Fort Sam Houston) and were sentenced to ten and twenty years in jail. It was, so far, the last train robbery to occur in the state of Texas.

The city continued to operate the choo-choo ride until 2001, when it was turned over to the San Antonio Zoo. "Old No. 99" was retired. The track was expanded to 24 inches to allow more passengers (though the loop shrank to two miles), and three new miniature locomotives appeared. These were copies of an 1863 Huntington steam locomotive. The "San Antonio Zoo Eagle" continues to make its daily runs (weather permitting) around Brackenridge Park.

Today the San Antonio Zoo has over a million visitors a year. Exhibit areas include the African Savanna, Gibbon Forest, Outpost Amazonia, Big Cat Valley, Cranes of the World, Africa Live, and Bear Corner.

The Zoological Society is also involved with a number of captive breeding and conservation programs for several different species including Black Rhino, Golden Lion Tamarin, Dama Gazelle, Attwater's Prairie Chicken, Black-Footed Ferret, and Andean Condor. One of the most active programs revolves around a species that once ranged naturally into south Texas until it was exterminated by humans—the Jaguar.

The Jaguar (*Panthera onca*) is the largest cat in the western hemisphere, weighing in at around 175 pounds. It is similar in many ways to the African and Asian Leopards (Jaguars can be distinguished from Leopards by the presence of smaller spots inside their larger spots). Pound for pound, Jaguars have the strongest bite force of any big cat, and they are ambush predators on large jungle herbivores such as Capybara and Tapirs, though they also eat a surprising amount of fish, and their jaws are powerful enough to penetrate the shells of river turtles and the bony skins of Caimans. While most cats kill their prey by clamping their jaws around the throat and suffocating it, Jaguars kill by driving their stout canine teeth through the victim's skull, penetrating the brain.

The evolutionary ancestors of the Jaguar crossed the ancient Beringia land bridge from Asia into Alaska and spread out from there. By the time Europeans arrived in the New World, the Jaguar was established from northern Argentina all the way up to the southern portions of Texas and Arizona. It prefers a habitat of rivercourses running through dense forest, but can also adapt to more open and drier grasslands. In the northern parts of the range, in Mexico and the United States, the cat's primary prey are Deer and Peccaries.

At one time there were as many as nine recognized subspecies (the population in Mexico and the southwest US was listed as the "American Jaguar"), but genetic analysis has led to the conclusion that all of the populations exchange genes and are all the same species. The famous "Black Panther" variety is not a subspecies, but is just an ordinary Jaguar with a genetic mutation that produces all-black fur (known as "melanism"). It is therefore possible for the same litter to contain both black and spotted individuals. (The same mutation occurs in African Leopards.) Like most cats, Jaguars are solitary except for brief periods during mating.

Today, the Jaguar is a conservation concern, and is listed as "threatened". Much of its forest range has been cleared for human use, and it is estimated that at least 50% of its former habitat has now been destroyed. The largest remaining Jaguar refuge, in the Amazon rainforest, is being jeopardized by logging and agriculture. In Mexico, the Jaguar's grassland habitat is also being fragmented and lost. Jaguars are poached throughout their range for their valuable and attractive hides.

In both Mexico and the United States, the cats were long targeted by hunters who viewed them as a threat to livestock.

The last Jaguar in southern California was seen in 1860, and by 1940 the last one was killed in Texas. Jaguars were considered to be extinct in the American Southwest.

During the 1960s, however, efforts were made to protect Jaguars by restricting the international fur trade and banning ranchers from killing them. As populations began to slowly recover, there were occasional reports—at first discounted—of wild Jaguars once again making their way from Mexico into the United States. An adult female was shot in Arizona in 1963, another Jaguar was killed two years later, and more were captured on film by camera traps in Texas, California and New Mexico. The Jaguar was apparently returning back to its former home in the United States. It was placed on the federal Endangered Species List and protected habitat areas were set aside, in cooperation with similar projects in northern Mexico. Although camera traps have only identified a small number of of individuals, biologists are hopeful that there may be more animals that are undetected, and they may even be breeding.

Zoos in North America began to draw up a Species Survival Plan for the Jaguar and hoped to use their captive population as a source of captive-bred cubs for eventual reintroduction to these protected areas. But it was found that of the 95 Jaguar individuals available in AZA-listed Zoos, only 22 could be traced back to the wild: the rest were bred from those, raising the issue of genetic inbreeding. So the SSP program calls for careful match-making between Zoo Jaguars to insure the highest possible genetic variability and the widest possible gene pool, supplemented by occasional individuals that are captured from the wild in South America as "nuisance animals" who have attacked livestock.

As part of the SSP, the San Antonio Zoo received a female Jaguar named "Arizona" from the Woodland Park Zoo in Seattle, to be mated with its male Jaguar "Balam". They produced a pair of cubs in September 2016.

BROOKFIELD ZOO
Chicago IL

By the first decades of the 20th century, Chicago was one of the largest cities in the US, a vital railroad hub, and a center of the meatpacking industry. It also had a reputation as a bare-knuckle brawler of a town, with a corrupt city government that catered to organized crime and bootleggers. By the end of World War One, Chicago was looking to soften its image.

So when Edith Rockefeller, daughter of one of the richest industrial dynasties in the world, married into the wealthy McCormick family and was given an 83-acre tract of land in the suburb of Brookfield IL as a wedding present, she in turn donated it to the Cook County Forest Preserve District, asking that they use it to develop a zoological garden to promote the city's image as a center for culture and education. The District added another 98 acres to the site and approached the city for cooperation in the project. They were supported by a collection of Chicago's prominent citizens, who in 1921 formed the nonprofit Chicago Zoological Society to lobby the city and the public for a Zoo.

And there things stalled. City support was scant until 1926, when a referendum vote agreed to impose a special county tax to be used to fund a Zoo. Those efforts were then crippled by the 1929 stock market crash, which eliminated fortunes overnight. As the Great Depression set in, local, state and federal officials now viewed the Zoo mostly as a public make-work project that could be used to keep a number of people employed.

Nevertheless, the Brookfield Zoo was one of the most innovative and far-reaching of its time. It was one of the first Zoos to be mapped out from the ground up using Carl Hagenbeck's new idea of spacious naturalistic open-air paddocks for the animals, separated by dry moats. Local architect Edwin Clark designed the administration buildings and the Reptile House, which were built by workers from the WPA. When the Zoo opened in July 1934, admission was free.

Over a million people visited in its first year. One of the original animals on display was Cookie the Cockatoo, who had been hatched the year before. He would live at the Zoo until his death in 2016 at age 83, making him one of the oldest known birds. By 1938, Brookfield had managed to obtain three rare Giant Pandas from China, known as Su-Lin, Mei-Mei and Mei-Lan. They quickly became a popular exhibit, though at the time there was little Zoo focus on conservation and there was no attempt to breed the Pandas, even though they were already becoming rare in the wild.

When the US entered World War Two in 1941, the city's financial support collapsed as well as visitorship, and the Zoo took to selling some of its animals to private collectors as a way of maintaining its budget. The postwar recovery gave Brookfield a temporary boost, and the Zoo completed several projects including the Children's Zoo, a veterinary hospital (one of the first in the US), and the Roosevelt Fountain (which honors conservationist President Teddy Roosevelt).

But the 1960s brought a period of neglect and budget cuts. The buildings fell into disrepair, and the quality of the Zoo steadily declined. Once again Chicago gained the image of a corrupt political fiefdom, and this was capped by the humiliation of the 1968 Democratic Party Convention, which was marred by riots and police violence. The whole world was watching Chicago, and it didn't like what it saw.

The embarrassed city once again made a conscious effort to improve its image, and that included modernizing the now-crumbling Zoo. The Cook County Forest Preserve District, which still owned the Zoo, issued a bond drive to raise funds, and the Zoo came under the management of the nonprofit Chicago Zoological Society. The outdoors enclosures were repaired and updated. A new Seven Seas Pavilion was added with a giant indoor Dolphin Pool, and Tropic World opened in three stages, featuring animals from Africa, Asia and South America. At the time, Tropic World was the largest indoor Zoo exhibit in the country.

George Rabb, who had worked for the Zoo as Curator of Research, was now hired as Director, and he turned the facility towards conservation and scientific work. Brookfield Zoo established a Conservation Biology Department to manage a variety of new programs, including a Declining Amphibian Populations Task Force and a reintroduction program for Golden Lion Tamarins. The Zoo also entered a partnership with Walt Disney World to establish a wildlife research center in Peru. Rabb himself came to head the Species Survival Commission, part of the International Union for the Conservation of Nature (IUCN). By 1990, Brookfield Zoo had improved its reputation as one of the worst Zoos in the country, to one of its best.

One of the species that the Zoo began to focus on was the Okapi, or Forest Giraffe.

The Okapi (*Okapia johnstoni*) is one of the most elusive of animals, and though large, is seldom seen in the wild. Its specialized habitat requirements—it prefers dense mountain rainforests—limit its range to just small areas of the Congo Basin in central Africa. Although the local Mbuti people hunted the animal, it was known in the rest of the world only by vague rumors and fantastic stories, which depicted the Okapi as some sort of unicorn. It wasn't until 1901 that British Governor Sir Harry Hamilton Johnston obtained two skins and a skull in Uganda and sent them to the British Museum in London for study.

The Okapi, it turned out, was not a unicorn after all, but a primitive relative of the Giraffe. Like the Giraffe, the Okapi has a long neck and extensible tongue which it uses to browse on tree leaves. But the Okapi is smaller in size and different in color, being covered with dense reddish-brown hair and vivid black and white stripes on the hindquarters.

The Okapi also differs in habitat. While the Giraffe is mostly a creature of the open savannah, Okapi are forest dwellers who like dense trees where there are fewer predators. Here they are so silent and well-camouflaged that the Congo natives refer to them as "the ghosts of the forest".

Because Okapi are so elusive and isolated, they are difficult to study and little is known about them. At one time they may have ranged across the Congo rainforest, but in modern times they are known only from Uganda and Zaire (now the Democratic Republic of the Congo), and they have not been seen in Uganda for such a long time that it is believed they are extinct there. Their primary range seems to be in the Ituri Forest, an area of roughly 63,000 square miles in the northeastern Congo drainage. Little information is available about their population and there has been some controversy over how numerous Okapi are in their native range (estimates range wildly from less than 5,000 to over 35,000), but since they are confined to just one geographic region and their population is believed to be declining, they are considered to be "range-limited" and have therefore been given "endangered" status to protect them. Their habitat area has been steadily shrinking due to forest clearing for agriculture and for mineral mining, while the Okapi themselves are illegally hunted for bush meat and also accidentally caught in snare traps set for other species like Bongo and Leopard.

In the wild, Okapi seem to be mostly solitary, pairing up only during mating. No one has observed the breeding process in the wild, but in Zoos, the newborn calves spend most of their time hidden in a nest of leaves and vegetation while the mother wanders off to feed. This apparently protects the young Okapi from Leopards, their primary predator. The youngsters grow quickly, and can be ready to breed as adults in as little as two or three years. In Zoos, individuals have lived as long as thirty years. Captive Okapi sometimes fight for dominance using kicks and neck-whipping, similar to Giraffes. It is not known if this also happens in the wild, or if it is just an artifact of living in a confined Zoo environment.

The Okapi has been legally protected in its native Ituri Forest since 1933. In 1987 the Okapi Conservation Project was formed to coordinate international efforts to protect and study the animals in the wild. In 1992, the local government set about one-fifth of the remaining forest area aside as the Okapi Wildlife Reserve, and there is also a protected population in Maiko National Park. The Ituri is the largest intact rainforest area still remaining in Africa. International efforts, however, have been hampered by political instability and by the long and bloody civil wars which have wracked the region.

Once the new species was discovered in 1901, every Zoo in the world wanted an Okapi for themselves, and expeditions trekked into the Congo to obtain them. Most of these failed, as the delicate animals did not tolerate the process of capture and shipping, and wild Okapi are vulnerable to infection by parasitic nematode worms. Only a few individuals survived the trip.

The Brookfield Zoo, however, was one of the first in the United States to successfully obtain Okapi for display, and the first captive-born calf, named "Mr G", was born at the Zoo in 1959. Since then, the Zoo has sponsored research in the wild and has participated in the Okapi's Species Survival Plan, in cooperation with the San Diego Zoo. Since the 1970s, both Zoos have produced about 90 captive-bred Okapi calves between them. The captive Okapi population has been spread to a large number of Zoos around the world—almost 50—as a way of protecting them against loss from disease or accident. The adults are shipped from Zoo to Zoo so pre-arranged matings can take place under the Species Survival Plan, which carefully calculates these meetings for maximum genetic diversity.

The Brookfield Zoo displays about 450 species. The exhibit areas include The Great Bears Wilderness, Australia, The Seven Seas, Pinniped Point, the Forest Preserve Nature Trail, Wolf Woods, the Hamill Family Play Zoo, and Habitat Africa. There was an attempt to open a Stingray Bay touch tank, but issues with the environmental controls during Chicago's freezing winters led to the deaths of several Cownose Rays and the display was closed.

In 1996 the Zoo briefly became the center of world attention, when a toddler accidentally fell into the gorilla pen in Tropic World. The crying child was picked up by Binti Jua, an adult female Lowland Gorilla, who protected him from the other gorillas and then took the toddler to her Zookeepers. The whole incident was captured on video and became a TV and YouTube sensation.

DALLAS ZOO
Dallas TX

In 1888, the city council in Dallas agreed to release $60 to purchase two Deer and two Cougars from a private seller and gave them to the Parks Department, which displayed them in a couple of pens in City Park. Over the years, the Dallas Zoo expanded as more animals were obtained, and in 1912 the entire collection was moved to Marsalis Park. There it continued to grow from 36 acres to its current 106. The famous big game hunter and adventurer Frank Buck captured many of the new animals from Africa and Asia.

Like many other Zoos, the Dallas Zoo underwent a series of modifications and repairs during the Great Depression. Dallas was, however, slow to adopt the concept of the open-air free-range enclosure, and many of its exhibits were still of the iron-bar type. It was also slow to join the rising conservation movement in the 1960s, and continued to retain its emphasis on exhibiting a large variety of individuals from different species. Nevertheless, the Zoo remained popular and its visitorship grew steadily.

By the 1980s, however, pressure was increasing for the Zoo to modernize—in particular, the AZA withheld its certification. By 1985, the city council had changed the Zoo's direction and the facility became a full partner in national and international conservation programs, and earned its AZA certification. The city issued two bond drives and raised $30 million for an expansion, and an entire new section was built, connected to the older exhibits by a tunnel.

The expansion was rapid. The Wilds of Africa area opened in 1990 and the Tiger Habitat in 1999, followed by the Giants of the Savannah in 2010 (funded by a $5 million private donation). The original exhibits were now known as ZooNorth. They contained Primate Place, the Bird and Reptile Building, the Wildlife Amphitheater, the Children's Zoo, and the Bug U exhibit.

A new city transportation route to the Zoo allowed easier access by the public. And in 2009, the city council turned the day-to-day management of the Zoo over to the nonprofit Dallas Zoological Society, which had been founded in 1955 to support the Zoo.

Today, the Zoo is a participant in over 40 different Species Survival Plans, ranging from the Arabian Oryx to the Wattled Cranes to Allen's Swamp Monkey. One of the species that the Zoo now works with is the Aruba Island Rattlesnake, which is considered to be one of the rarest and most endangered snakes in the world.

Little attention was paid to snake conservation until the 1980s, when the AZA took an interest and formed an Advisory Group to evaluate the status of endangered snakes and evaluate the potential for any successful captive breeding programs. They selected a list of around a dozen candidate species.

The familiar rattlesnakes are unique to the New World, though they are related to the Old World vipers. They range from the Canadian border all the way to Chile and Argentina, though the greatest variety is found in the American West. In South America the most common species is the Neotropical Rattlesnake, also known as the Cascabel.

On the tiny island of Aruba, off the coast of Venezuela, is the Aruba Island Rattlesnake, which used to be considered a subspecies of the Cascabel but is now classified as a species of its own, *Crotalus unicolor*. First discovered and described in 1887, this is a smallish snake, with adults reaching 3-4 feet. It varies in color from light tan to a pale pink, with a series of darker diamond-shaped markings along its back.

Like all rattlers, the Aruba Island snake carries a rattle on its tail. This is made from dead dried skin, and consists of a series of interlocking segments, with a new section added each time the snake sheds its skin. When the snake is angry or annoyed, it rapidly vibrates the tip of its tail, which makes the segments knock against each other and produces the distinctive rapid buzzing sound that characterizes rattlesnakes. The Aruba snake's rattle tends to be somewhat smaller than most.

Drop for drop, the Aruba Island Rattlesnake has some of the most potent venom of any viperid snake. But on its island home, the snakes do not have any serious threats from predators and are therefore pretty calm and placid. The venom serves mostly to procure food. Although the Aruba rattlers will eat small mammals and birds, the primary prey seems to be the Whiptail Lizards which inhabit the island.

Rattlesnakes, along with Copperheads and Cottonmouths, are "pit vipers", and possess a specialized sensory organ on their face which detects the infrared heat that is radiated by warm-blooded prey. This helps the snakes find food even at night, and blindfolded pit vipers are still able to accurately strike prey using only their pit sensors. Like all snakes, they cannot chew and must swallow their prey whole, and by dislocating their jaw joints they are able to down prey that is much wider than they are.

Unlike most snakes, which lay eggs, rattlesnakes deliver live young who are capable of hunting and living on their own from birth. The newborns lack rattles, however—they have only a single silent segment at the end of their tail called a "button". Youngsters therefore cannot rattle until they have shed a few times and added some segments. Litter size ranges from 5-15 young at a time. The adults reach maturity in about 5 years, and the typical lifespan is about 20 years.

The ancestors of the Aruba Island Rattlesnake were probably individuals of the Cascabel species which floated across the stretch of water from the mainland to the island on logs or mats of vegetation, perhaps during the many tropical storms that sweep the area. Over geological time, the snakes evolved to become specialized for island life. They became smaller as a response to the relatively less abundant prey population, and in the absence of any predators of their own they became less belligerent and defensive than their Cascabel cousins. It is a well-known phenomenon for island species to be smaller and more placid than their mainland ancestors—an adaptation known as "island dwarfism".

As island species adapt to their isolated environments, they have a tendency to become specialized in a variety of different ecological niches. This can produce a large number of new species that are not found anywhere else, a trend known as "adaptive radiation". This also leaves the new species extremely vulnerable to any ecological disruption, however, such as a climate change or the introduction of a new predator.

In the case of the Aruba Island Rattlesnake, this new "predator" is humans. Aruba is a tropical paradise for tourists, and humans have now covered most of the island with houses, hotels, and travel destinations. The effect on the snakes has been devastating, and as humans have taken over, the Rattlesnake has been pushed into a tiny refuge at the southern tip of the island, where it has nowhere else to go. As a result, it is estimated that there are only around 250 of the snakes remaining on the island, making it one of the rarest reptiles in the world.

Many people, of course, don't like snakes anyway and wouldn't really care if they disappear. But snakes are vital links in the world's ecosystems. Since they are right in the middle of the food web, being mid-sized predators on small prey animals as well as being prey themselves for larger predators, snakes and other reptiles make up a large portion of the food chain. Without them, the entire natural system would unravel.

Efforts to preserve and protect the rattlesnake began in the 1980s. The government of Aruba set aside 12 square miles of the snake's remaining habitat (about one-fifth of the island's total land area) as Arikok National Park, and a nonprofit group called WildAruba was formed to educate the public about the need to protect the island's unique wildlife. Zoos in South America and the United States set up an assurance collection which would insure the survival of the species even if it disappeared from the wild, and drew up a Species

Survival Plan in 1982 for captive-breeding (the first one established for any snake species).

Today there are around 100 Aruba Island Rattlesnakes being held by a number of Zoos, including the Toledo Zoo, Jacksonville Zoo, and Dallas Zoo. Some of these are being maintained and distributed as an assurance colony, and the others are part of the captive breeding program. In Aruba, the snakes have become the basis for a local ecotourism industry around Arikok National Park.

Survival Plan in 1982, for captive-breeding Bali mynahs, a thickly-crested...

Today, there are around 600 Arabs Oryxes Rothschilds going wild in a number of zoos, and being that led to the Jerusalem Zoo and Tel... Now being in gross confusing... ...a... destruction of in a scientists... ...a... ...a... ...be one... the a... comeback...

ZOO ATLANTA
Atlanta GA

In March 1889, the circus came to Atlanta. The city was just beginning to recover from the destruction that had been wreaked upon it during the Civil War, when Union forces under General Ulysses S Grant had defeated the Confederates. The circus provided a few nights of much-needed entertainment.

Unfortunately, this circus was in dire financial straits, and it finally expired. Unpaid employees walked off the job and went home, leaving behind abandoned equipment and all the caged animals from the traveling menagerie. Atlanta officials ended up confiscating the whole mess and putting it up for public auction.

Local businessman George V Gress purchased the entire menagerie, containing four Lions, a Jaguar, Hyena, Black Bear, Raccoon, Elk, Gazelle, Mexican Wild Boar, Lion, Cougar, Camel and a couple snakes, and donated them all to the city. They were moved, cages and all, from the railroad yards to Grant Park, the town's largest green space (which had been named after the Confederate officer who designed the city's defenses during the war, not after that other guy). It became the Grant Park Zoo. With community support, the new Zoo was expanded as more animals were added from donations, including an Elephant named Clio in 1890.

Forty-five years later, a local businessman named Asa Candler Jr (whose father had founded the Coca-Cola Company) was having animal troubles of his own. He was keeping a large private collection of exotic "pets" at his swank estate on Briarcliff Road, including a Tiger, a Leopard, Zebras, Water Buffalo, a Hyena, Sea Lions, Llamas, Bears, and an Elephant. His wealthy neighbors tolerated Candler's eccentric hobby until he had a series of escapes, when they complained to the city. Candler worked out a deal: he would donate his entire collection to the Zoo, if they agreed to build a series of new pens and cages for them. At a stroke, the Grant Park Zoo nearly doubled in size. The tiny Zoo (with its tiny budget) was not really prepared for this, and struggled to keep up with the unexpected expansion.

For the next several decades, city support for the Zoo waxed and waned, and the Zoo's fortunes along with it. At various times, the city council wanted to cut the budget, or perhaps close the Grant Park Zoo altogether and use the money for other things. And each time, prominent businessmen or wealthy society patrons would step in with a contribution to keep the Zoo going.

In the 1950s and 60s the Zoo underwent modifications, beginning the process of replacing its iron-bar cages with modern open-air paddocks, and new Director John Roth began to focus more attention on conservation and public eduction. In 1970, the nonprofit Atlanta Zoological Society was founded to support the Zoo and help raise money for more improvements.

But during the 1970s the city of Atlanta faced serious financial difficulty and its support for the Zoo fell as budgets were slashed. The Zoo steadily declined: many of the animals, especially the cats and primates, were still being kept in substandard indoors iron-bar cells, and many of the buildings required repair work. Newspapers told the story of Willie B, the Gorilla who had been born at the Zoo in 1961, spent all his time inside a cage, and had never been outdoors. By 1984 the national Sunday-newspaper supplement "Parade" named Atlanta one of the "Top 10 Worst Zoos in the Country", and shortly later the AZA pulled the Zoo's accreditation. There were public calls to shut the Zoo down completely.

The city was shamed into acting. The Zoo had always been free to the public, but now an admissions charge was enacted to help put the institution on a more stable financial footing. A nonprofit company called Atlanta Fulton County Zoo, Inc. was formed to run the facility with the cooperation of the Zoological Society and with new Zoo Director Terry Maple. All of these changes were reflected in a new name: Zoo Atlanta.

With city support from Mayor Andrew Young in the form of a $50 million grant, another donation from the Ford Motor Company, and with outreach and fundraising programs to the public, the Zoo began expanding. Flamingo Plaza and the Wildlife Theater were later joined by the African Rain Forest, Mzima Springs and Masai Mara exhibit areas. A group of Gorillas was loaned by the Yerkes Primate Center, and in 1990 the Zoo obtained two Giant Pandas from China. The once-disgraced Zoo had undergone a remarkable transformation, and was now listed as one of the "Top 10 Best Zoos in the Country".

Today, Zoo Atlanta focuses heavily on protecting wildlife and educating the public on conservation issues. The "Trader's Alley: Wildlife's Fading Footprints" exhibit illustrates the impact that international trade, legal and illegal, has on animals and their habitats. Of the 220 species kept at Zoo Atlanta, around 20 are the center of SSP captive-breeding efforts, including the Giant Panda, Bali Mynah, Orangutan, Bongo, and King Vulture.

The King Vulture (*Sarcoramphus papa*) ranges from Mexico down through Central America to northern Argentina. (There was one report of a King Vulture in Florida in the 1770s, but none have been seen since, and this one is now considered to be a mistake, a misidentification, or perhaps an erratic who was accidentally blown in on a storm.) The body feathers are mostly black and white, the neck is, like most vultures, bare and unfeathered, and the head is spectacularly splotched with bright red, yellow and orange, with a prominent fleshy crest. One odd quirk is that this species, uniquely among vultures, lacks eyelashes.

Fossils show that relatives of the King Vulture lived in South America some three million years ago, but they are extinct now and the *S. papa* species is the only one remaining. The large birds were familiar figures to the Mayan and Aztec natives of Central America who often depicted them in their written pictographs, referring to the vultures as *"cozcacuauhtli"*, meaning "collared eagle". In some myths, King Vultures served as messengers from the gods.

King Vultures are the third-largest of the six species of American vultures, with a wingspan of up to seven feet. Only the California and Andean Condors are larger. Although the New World vultures are very similar in appearance and lifestyle to the Old World vultures in Africa and Asia, they are not very closely related: the New World vultures are believed to be descendants of storks, while Old World vultures are classed with hawks and eagles. The similarities between the Old World and New World birds are the result of "convergent evolution", in which different groups adopt the same body plans and lifestyle behaviors in response to similar environmental conditions.

Not very much is known about King Vultures in the wild. They prefer habitats of lowland rainforest with nearby patches of wetlands, where they inhabit the tops of the tallest trees. They spend most of their time riding thermal air currents with wings outstretched, covering long distances without needing to flap their wings. In this way, the birds can act as nature's "cleanup crew", watching for recently dead animals and removing these potential sources of disease and contamination. Unlike many vultures, King Vultures seem to have a poor sense of smell, and locate their food by sight—often they are attracted by smaller vulture species circling around a potential food item. Although they are large birds, King Vultures do not kill any prey of their own and are completely dependent upon leftover food that has been abandoned by other predators.

When they find the remains of a Jaguar kill or other carcass, the King Vultures glide down to the ground, drive away any smaller scavengers, and use their large strong beak to tear off edible portions of meat and skin. Since they are usually late to a predator kill, King Vultures tend to specialize by feeding on the dried-out skin and flesh that have been left behind by other scavengers. In some instances, however, in the case of a natural death, the King Vulture may be the only scavenger strong enough to tear through the hide of a recently-dead animal, and the other scavengers need to wait for the larger birds to arrive and tear a way into the body. The naked neck and head allows the birds to poke inside body cavities and prevents them from being caked with blood or rotting meat. Vultures have powerful digestive juices in their stomach which is strong enough to dissolve bones, and allows them to eat dead rotting flesh without danger of infection by bacteria.

The legs are also bare of feathers, and like most other vultures the King Vulture is able to cool itself off in hot weather by urinating on its legs and feet, which evaporates and carries off heat.

Since the birds are inaccessible and difficult to study in their remote rainforest habitats, most of what we know about their behavior comes from captive individuals. King Vultures are mostly solitary, though they will peaceably gather around a large kill to feed together. Breeding begins with an elaborate courtship ritual which involves loud snorting, hissing, and heavy breathing. Like most vultures, they seem to mate for life.

Instead of making a nest like most birds, however, mated King Vultures lay their single egg inside a soft rotted hollow in a tree trunk or stump. This will hatch in about two months, with both parents taking turns in incubating the egg and then in feeding the chick, which they do by carrying bits of meat in their crop and regurgitating it. The snowy white chick grows quickly. It can fly at around 3 months, will molt into adult plumage at around 18 months, and be ready to breed at 3-4 years. The adults can live for over 30 years.

Although King Vultures are found in a wide area, their population is believed to be declining and they are now protected by the CITES treaty, and although they are listed by the IUCN as a "Species of Least Concern" they are the subject of a captive-breeding program under their own Species Survival Plan. With their large size and spectacular colors, the birds are also a favorite with the public, and a number of King Vultures are bred specifically for transfer to other Zoos as an exhibit, where they serve as "animal ambassadors" to educate visitors without the need to take any individuals from the wild.

The Atlanta Zoo's resident King Vulture is an adult female named "Roswell". She has been mated with male birds from the Zoo in Salt Lake City and the Riverbanks Zoo in South Carolina. Atlanta also temporarily housed the Riverbanks Zoo's resident pair, Venus and Lilith, while their enclosure was being remodeled.

ZOO MIAMI
Miami FL

In the years before the Second World War, Florida had already undergone drastic changes. Once a sparsely-populated tropical land of orange groves and cattle ranches, the state wasn't connected to the rest of the United States until the 1910s when a system of railroads was installed. The effect was instant. During the Roaring Twenties, cities like Miami, Tampa, and Jacksonville doubled in size, then tripled. Winter advertisements in northern newspapers featured photos of luxury hotels with beach babe "flappers" cavorting on the sand in daring above-the-knee bathing suits. Even gangster Al Capone had a winter mansion in Florida.

Land prices skyrocketed. Speculators from up north flooded in, buying up whatever land was available—often sight unseen—and reselling it for immense profits. The Florida land bubble, however, was simply unsustainable. Land prices reached such astronomical levels that new buyers, upon which the entire speculative edifice rested, could no longer be found. Hurricanes in 1926 and 1928, which did extensive damage to the Miami area, didn't help. Even before the 1929 stock market crash, the Florida real estate bubble had already popped. People who had purchased property on credit now found themselves hopelessly in debt, real estate millionaires became destitute overnight, and cities like Miami that depended on property tax revenue faced collapsing budgets.

In 1940, the Matheson family, which owned one of the largest coconut plantations in the United States, cut a deal with the local Miami-Dade county government: the family would donate some 900 acres of its land on Key Biscayne, almost half the island, as a public park, if the county agreed to build a causeway from the Miami mainland to allow automobile traffic. Not coincidentally, this would greatly increase the value of the land still held by the family, but the county agreed to the plan, and the donated land became Crandon Park. Construction of the causeway was delayed by World War Two, but was finally completed in 1947.

The following year, a small traveling animal menagerie was performing in Miami when one of its trucks broke down. The managers did not have enough extra money to pay for the repairs, so they traded three Monkeys, two Bears and a Goat to the garage owner, who in turn donated them to the county government. A series of cages was constructed at Crandon Park to hold them, and within a short time the county officially set aside a 48-acre tract for the Crandon Park Zoo.

After the Second World War, the United States experienced an economic boom, and Florida once again became the center of the tourist industry. This was fueled by two major improvements: the interstate highway system now allowed easy access by car from across the country, and the spread of air conditioning made Florida's tropical paradise a comfortable mecca for travelers. Tourist attractions appeared everywhere: tropical gardens, Alligator wrestling and roadside snake farms, glass-bottom boat river tours and "jungle cruises", fake Native American villages, fishing charters, and orange tree groves.

And one of the most popular destinations for visitors to Miami was the Crandon Park Zoo. By 1960, the Zoo had grown steadily. It now contained over 1,000 animals and was one of the largest exhibits in the United States. A miniature train ride took tourists on a 1.5-mile loop around the Park. But criticism was also mounting. The public's perception of "zoos" had changed, and Crandon Park had not kept up. The environmentalist movement had increased people's awareness, and the facility's cement and iron-bar cages were now considered cruel and outdated. Some newspapers called for rebuilding and modernizing the Zoo; others called for closing it down.

Mother Nature unexpectedly made the decision in September 1965. Hurricane Betsy swept across Florida before moving up the Gulf of Mexico to Louisiana. Miami was especially hard hit, and the Crandon Park Zoo was inundated with a storm surge exceeding three feet. The damage was extensive: the bird aviary was nearly destroyed, roofs were torn off the buildings, and over one-fourth of the Zoo's entire animal collection was killed.

It took nearly two years for the Zoo to recover. By 1967 the collection was back up to around 1200 animals. In 1968, Crandon Park received two rare white Bengal Tigers, and a pair of Indian Rhinos shortly later. In 1973, the Zoo became the first institution in the US to breed Bald Eagles, which were endangered in the wild by DDT poisoning and had become a symbol of the conservation movement.

But county and city officials had already decided that the Zoo needed a new beginning. When the US Navy closed its Richmond Naval Air Station on the outskirts of Miami, the city immediately bought the land and began making plans to relocate the Zoo there, in a brand new facility. The new area covered 750 acres, which would make it the largest Zoo in the United States, and allow for spacious outdoors free-range enclosures for the animals and lots of room for up-to-date buildings for veterinary care and food preparation. The new Miami MetroZoo would be one of the most modern Zoos in the world.

Construction began in 1975, and the new Zoo opened in 1980 with 38 exhibits covering 200 acres. This would expand over the years to 324 acres. Exhibit areas would grow to include 3,000 individual animals from 500 species, with sections displaying specimens from Africa, Asia, Australia, South America, and a large collection of Florida natives. There was a setback in 1992 when Hurricane Andrew destroyed the Aviary and uprooted most of the landscaping, but by the time of the 30th anniversary celebration in 2010, the Zoo, now renamed Zoo Miami, was ranked as one of the Top Ten in the

US, and was expanded further with a new $43 million Mission Everglades exhibit.

Because the Zoo was spread over a wide area, it offered several options for visitors to get around during Florida's hot tropical summer days. There were several miles of paved walkways that threaded through all the exhibits. For the less hardy, there were rentable "Quad-Cycles" which allowed groups of up to 6 adults and two children to pedal their way along the level pathways in shaded cycle-carts. There were also motorized trams that gave narrated tours of the entire Zoo. And for the ultimate in comfort, the air-conditioned Monorail offered narrated tours.

Zoo Miami also became heavily involved in conservation projects and captive breeding, and sponsored a number of education and outreach projects focused on the nearby Everglades, especially the endangered Key Deer. The Zoo was one of the founders of the Butterfly Conservation Initiative, a nationwide program to encourage protection of habitat for endangered North American butterflies including the Monarch. And as part of its conservation fund, the Zoo now finances facilities in Thailand for captive-breeding and rehabilitation of the endangered Clouded Leopard.

The Clouded Leopard (*Neofelis nebulosa*) is an elusive and secretive cat that ranges from the Himalayas across southeast Asia to Indonesia and up to China. The Leopard was first described in 1821 from the skin of a cat that was obtained in China and exhibited in a London menagerie until it died. Later specimens from Nepal and Taiwan were described as separate species, but in 1867 these were all grouped together as a single taxon. In 2006, however, the populations in Sumatra and Borneo were split off into a different species, *Neofelis diardi*, known as the Sunda Clouded Leopard, with each island containing a distinct subspecies.

Clouded Leopards are often considered to be the smallest of the "big cats", with adult males weighing around 50 pounds. The name comes from the wide cloud-like splotches on the pelt.

In the wild, these are solitary cats. The Leopard's preferred habitat is thick lowland rainforest or mangrove swamps, and it is specially adapted to living in trees. The paws are wide and the toes are padded, enabling the cat to grip branches, and specially-adapted rotating bones in the ankle allow Clouded Leopards to grip tree trunks and climb up or down headfirst. The tail is also exceptionally long and acts as a balancing rod when the Leopard moves along a tree branch. Although these cats do most of their hunting on the ground, they shelter in trees to avoid larger predators such as Tigers which may share their habitat. They are sometimes called "Monkey Cats".

Another unusual trait is the greatly elongated canine teeth, which are proportionately longer than any other feline species, and jaws that have an extraordinarily wide gape. This may allow for a better grip on small quick prey like birds. The primary quarry for Clouded Leopards are monkeys, birds and rodents, but being relatively strong for their size they can also tackle larger prey like small deer or wild pigs.

Since Clouded Leopards are very secretive, it is difficult to study them in the wild, and not much is known about them. They appear to be mostly nocturnal, though this may be a predator-avoidance strategy since they seem to be more active during the day in areas where there are no Tigers sharing their range. The Leopards are solitary animals, with males and females joining only for mating.

Although Zoos in the United States were keeping Clouded Leopards as early as the 1940s, there was no effort to breed them until the 1970s, when a Species Survival Plan was drawn up. Breeding the cats has proven to be difficult, however, as very little is known about their mating habits in the wild. In most cats, ovulation in the female is stimulated during the act of mating, but the Clouded Leopard is unusual in that it often ovulates spontaneously, at random times. This has made artificial insemination virtually impossible (though the Nashville Zoo, in cooperation with the Smithsonian, successfully carried out the procedure in 2017). The breeding program is therefore dependent on bringing males and females from different Zoos together.

But this presents serious difficulties of their own. In captive conditions, the males are often aggressive towards the smaller females, and attempts to keep them together led to fights that sometimes resulted in deaths. Over time it was found that immature males were less hostile, especially if they were allowed to spend time with the female to form a bond prior to sexual maturity. As a result, Zoos now establish their breeding pairs by introducing very young males to adult females, who then grow up together for a year or two until the male is ready to mate. Once a mating pair is established, it is then maintained.

If kittens are born, there is yet another difficulty. Under captive conditions, the female Leopards are inclined to reject and abandon their young, which forces the Zookeepers to intervene and raise the babies by hand. This has the effect of imprinting the youngsters onto humans, making them unsuitable for release into the wild. These human-raised Clouded Leopards are therefore usually trained to act as "animal ambassadors" for educational talks and shows.

All of this has made captive-breeding very difficult, and although a number of Zoos around the world display Clouded Leopards, births are somewhat rare and celebrated events. And when the Zoo Miami produced two cubs in February 2020 which were successfully nursed by their mother, they were faced with an additional difficulty: the Covid-19 pandemic began to rage just a few weeks later, and felines are vulnerable to the coronavirus. The Zoo therefore had to take extensive steps to isolate the youngsters from humans as much as possible to avoid exposure to the virus.

LOS ANGELES ZOO
Los Angeles, CA

In 1882, a wealthy mine-owner named Griffith J Griffith (yes, that was his name) decided to get into the real estate business, and purchased a number of housing developments in Los Angeles near the Santa Monica Mountains. He also opened up a large Ostrich ranch—the feathers were being used in ladies' hats and were very valuable. Griffith did well, became a respected citizen, and donated 3,000 acres of his property to the city as a public park. It would later become the site of an astronomical observatory and an early airfield used by aviation pioneer Glenn Martin.

The city of Los Angeles, meanwhile, had opened its first Zoo in 1885. This was a small collection of around a dozen animals, including Ostriches and Alligators, along an artificial pond in Eastlake Park in east LA (later renamed Lincoln Park). Starved of funding and with few visitors, however, the tiny Eastlake Zoo struggled, and faced constant criticism from the *Los Angeles Times*, which editorialized against the deplorable conditions and declared, "The present quarters for the animals are anything but satisfactory". In 1912, the city decided to close Eastlake and move all the animals to a new Zoo.

They chose a spot in Griffith Park, where Griffith's now-defunct Ostrich ranch had been. Here a series of cement cells fronted by iron bars were constructed, holding about 15 animals that were relocated from Eastlake Park. The new Griffith Park Zoo officially opened later in 1912.

By this time, the section of Los Angeles known as Hollywood was already becoming a center for the new silent film industry. One of the early pioneers was William Selig, who specialized in "wild animal" films. These were shot using Selig's own personal collection of exotic animals in Eastlake, which grew to become one of the largest in the country. His silent films were enormously successful, and his studio retained a pool of animal trainers, zookeepers and staff.

But in 1925, Selig sold his assortment of animals. Most of them went to the Griffith Park Zoo. The rest were gathered in Luna Park and became the California Zoological Gardens, which made its money by renting out animals for Hollywood film productions. "Zoo Park", as it became known, weathered the Great Depression, but in 1940 a flood damaged many of the buildings and the company faced a slowdown in movie productions. The entire stock of exotic animals—worth over $1 million—was sold at auction. Many went to private buyers. A few were obtained by Griffith Park.

The Griffith Park Zoo, meanwhile, had been expanded during the Depression with Federal money and workers from the Works Progress Administration (WPA), and was now receiving 2 million visitors per year, including a stream of Hollywood movie stars and studio moguls. Nevertheless, it was neglected by the city and steadily fell into disrepair, and newspapers once again condemned the public Zoo, calling it "inadequate, ugly, poorly designed, and under-financed".

In 1958, the city decided once again to start all over with a brand new Zoo. Using an $8 million bond issue, a new 133-acre site was selected in Griffith Park about two miles away, at the place where the old Aerodrome used to be. This time, the Zoo was designed from the ground up as a modern facility with open-air enclosures and a focus on naturalistic settings. (At Griffith Park Zoo, the old cement animal cells were left open, with picnic tables and a hiking trail, as a reminder of how bad the Zoo had once been.) In 1963, the nonprofit Greater Los Angeles Zoo Association (GLAZA) was formed as a "friends of the Zoo" citizens group which helped with fundraising and support.

The Los Angeles Zoo opened in November 1966. The opening ceremony featured speeches by the Mayor and GLAZA officials, and a performance by the LA Symphony Orchestra. In 1971, GLAZA held a "Primate Ball" fundraising party to raise money for a new monkey and great ape exhibit. It was a star-studded affair with Ed McMahon emceeing and a guest list including Lucille Ball and Gregory Peck. Renamed the "Beastly Ball", it continued as an annual fundraiser for the Zoo, with contributions running over $1 million a year.

The new Zoo was intended from the start to be heavily involved with conservation and education efforts. Shortly after it opened, the Zoo received two rare Harpy Eagles from Peru and Ecuador, and produced the first eaglets to be hatched in the United States. When the captive breeding program for the California Condor was launched, the Los Angeles Zoo was heavily involved. Working with other Zoos, LA bred a number of Arabian Oryx that were returned to the wild at the Hai-Bar Reserve in Israel, and later a colony of Golden Lion Tamarins was reintroduced to the Poco das Antas Reserve in Brazil. This was followed by a herd of Mountain Bongos that were resettled in the Mount Kenya Game Ranch.

Another species that has been bred at the Zoo is the Komodo Dragon. At ten feet in length, the Komodo Dragon (*Varanus komodensis*) is the largest living species of lizard in the world, and has long been the source of myth, story and legend.

Komodo Dragons are part of the large Varanid family of monitor lizards, which are widespread across tropical areas of Asia, Africa, Australia and South America. The Dragons, however, are found only on the Indonesian island of Komodo and a few surrounding islets including Rintja, Padar and Flores. Here, safe from mammalian competitors, the lizards have evolved as top predator and reached a giant size.

By the 19th century, Indonesia was a Dutch colony, part of the Netherland East Indies. It was an exotic and little-known place, where unknown species were routine and where a Dutch Army officer would find "Java Man", an ancient fossil human who would revolutionize the scientific world. Spice traders from the famous Dutch East India Company had long heard tales and stories from natives of huge "dragons" or "land crocodiles" known locally as *Ora* that lived on some of the islands, but these were usually dismissed as tall tales and exaggerations, perhaps centered on the local Water Monitor lizard, which could itself reach six feet in length.

It wasn't until 1910 that Lieutenant van Steyn van Hensbroek, an official in the local Dutch colonial government, accompanied an expedition to Komodo to investigate the stories. Encountering the fabled *Ora* for himself, van Steyn managed to obtain a photograph of a living lizard and shot another one, sending the skin to Peter Ouwens, Director of the colonial Zoological Museum in Java. Ouwens in turn managed to obtain two more dead specimens from natives, and wrote up a scientific paper in 1912 which formally described the species.

The paper caused a sensation, and now every Zoo in the world wanted a Komodo Dragon. The first to get them was the Bronx Zoo, which in 1926 sent adventurer W. Douglas Burden to Indonesia to obtain them. He came back with a dozen dead Komodo Dragons and two live ones, which were displayed at the Zoo but unfortunately only lived a short time. Another expedition from England captured two Dragons which went on exhibit at the London Zoo a year later. Meanwhile, Burden wrote a book about his exciting exploits in the Indonesian jungle, laced with breathless prose of danger and derring-do. A few years later, Burden's account inspired a Hollywood screenwriter to produce a cinematic story about a giant ape that lived in a jungle-covered island inhabited by prehistoric beasts. It became "King Kong".

The Dutch colonial authorities, meanwhile, realized that their Dragons were now a valuable commodity, and they took steps to protect them. Outside expeditions were banned, the export of Dragons was outlawed, and only a tiny number of the giant lizards were captured for scientific research.

Fortunately, the isolated islands where the *Ora* lived were left untouched by the chaos of the Second World War, and when Indonesia won its independence the new government continued the legal restrictions protecting the species. In 1969, biologist Walter Auffenberg, accompanied by Indonesian partner Putra Sastrawan, was allowed to spend 11 months on Komodo studying the Dragons. They tagged, tracked and followed some 50 of the lizards. In 1980 Komodo National Park was established, which encloses and protects most of the lizard's remaining habitat.

The Varanid family of monitor lizards seems, on the basis of fossil evidence, to have appeared in Asia some 40 million years ago and spread out from there. They were related to the extinct Cretaceous mosasaurs, which were not dinosaurs but large sea-going lizards. Varanids also share some skull characteristics with snakes, and may share a common ancestor. Monitor lizards have more efficient respiratory and circulatory systems than most reptiles, which allows them to be much more active and energetic.

There is some indication that the Komodo Dragon species in particular evolved in Australia, and migrated to the Indonesian islands during the last Ice Age, when sea levels were lower. As the ice sheets melted and sea levels rose again, the Dragons became trapped on their isolated islands.

Komodo Dragons are ambush predators who lie in wait at waterholes or along trails and lunge out at prey that happens to pass by. They are also capable of sprinting at a surprisingly fast speed for short distances. Most of their prey consists of wild Deer, Goats, or Pigs, but a large Dragon is capable of bringing down even Water Buffalo.

For many years, it was thought that the *Ora* were able to kill their prey with a single bite using toxins generated by bacteria in their mouth, and would then use their acute sense of smell to track the victim after it died from septicemia. Today, however, we know this is incorrect. Studies have shown that the Dragons actually have a pair of venom glands inside their lower jaw which oozes a mildly paralytic venom into the bite. This seems to stun the prey while it is being ripped apart by the Dragon's powerful jaws.

So far, the conservation of wild Komodo Dragons in the national parks seems to be successful, and populations seem to be stable. But the extremely limited geographic range of the lizards makes them vulnerable to a chance event like a typhoon or epidemic which could wipe out an entire island. Therefore, most of the captive breeding programs are aimed at establishing an assurance collection which insures that if the Dragons suffer some sort of disaster in the wild, there is enough captive population available to breed them back into existence.

Today, around 50 Zoos worldwide have Komodo Dragons, including about 35 in the US. Many of these are descended from a pair of lizards that the government of Indonesia gifted to the Smithsonian National Zoo in 1964. Since 2010, the Los Angeles Zoo has had four successful clutches and has raised 53 Dragons to maturity. Most of these were placed in other Zoos as educational "animal ambassadors".

Despite the LA Zoo's success with its conservation programs and despite a steady visitorship, the city once again began to neglect the Zoo in the 1980s, and its infrastructure began a slow decline. In January 1992, one of the water mains inside the Zoo failed, which cut off water to half of the Zoo grounds. The City Council had already been writing up a new Master Plan to use a total of $300 million over ten years to expand and update the Zoo, and now they passed an emergency fund to fix some of the infrastructure issues.

It wasn't enough, and when the AZA threatened to revoke the Zoo's accreditation, the city finally passed a series of funding bills and bond issues by public referendum. The existing facilities were upgraded, and a long series of additions came along. The new Children's Zoo opened in 2001, followed over the years by the Gottlieb Animal Health and Conservation Center veterinary hospital, the Children's Discovery Center educational classrooms, the Elephants of Asia paddock, and the Rainforest of the Americas exhibit.

The Los Angeles Zoo is now recognized as one of the best in California.

ZOO TAMPA
Tampa FL

For much of its history, the Lowry Park Zoo (now known as Zoo Tampa) struggled with issues stemming from lack of funding and support. Today, however, the Zoo has undergone an amazing transformation and is one of the leading Zoos in Florida.

During the 1930s, the City of Tampa amassed a small collection of wild animals that had been donated by local citizens, and these were housed at a makeshift exhibit in Plant Park, on the grounds of the University of Tampa. There were Alligators, Raccoons, and local birds. Many of these had been captured by animal-control officers in people's backyards.

By 1955, the informal Zoo was beginning to outgrow its available space, and Mayor Nick Nuccio proposed moving the entire collection to Lowry Park and placing it under the management of the city Parks Department. Lowry Park had been established on the Hillsborough River in 1925 and was already the site of Fairyland, a children's park containing statues of nursery rhyme figures. "Lowry Park Zoo" opened in 1957.

Sadly, however, the city was fairly stingy with the funding, and although the Zoo received some donations (Sumter Lowry Jr, the son of the City Commissioner for whom the park had been named, donated enough money to buy an Elephant and construct a bandstand), for the most part it was severely underfunded. In an attempt to attract more visitors, the park added a skyride and a roller coaster, but over the years the lack of money led to a steady decline as the obsolete concrete pens and barred animal cages fell into disrepair. The Humane Society condemned Lowry Park as "one of the worst zoos in America".

Finally in 1981 the city's Citizens Advisory Board publicly called for improvements to the Zoo. Mayor Bob Martinez committed $8 million in funding, and the nonprofit Lowry Park Zoo Association, made up of local citizens and businesses, raised another $20 million. After six years of fundraising efforts, the Zoo was closed for a major makeover.

When Lowry Park Zoo re-opened in March 1988, it was a completely different facility. The barred animal cells were gone, replaced by spacious enclosures with low stone walls. The birds were housed in a large netted free-flight Aviary, a new Primate World featured open paddocks for the monkeys and apes, and Asian Domain followed the modern idea of displaying animals in naturalistic settings that reflected their ecological and geographic relationships. There was also a Children's Petting Zoo. The revamped Zoo received over half a million visitors, and obtained its AZA accreditation a year later.

Management of the Zoo was transferred from the city Parks Department to the nonprofit Lowry Park Zoological Society. The city continued to fund the Zoo, however, and with this support the Zoological Society continue to raise money for expansions and improvements. The Lykes Florida Wildlife Center displayed native wildlife. The Wallaroo Station exhibited animal species from Australia, and the large Safari Africa area contained Elephants, Okapi, and other species. Stingray Bay allowed visitors to pet some of Florida's native stingrays. The Zoo more than doubled in size, and to reflect the expanding role, the name was formally changed to "Zoo Tampa" in 2018.

There were some growing pains. In 2006 one of the Zoo's Sumatran Tigers escaped from her cage and, when she charged a veterinarian who was trying to tranquilize her, she had to be shot. Two years later, a group of Patas Monkeys escaped from Safari Wild, a for-profit animal park that was owned by Zoo Tampa Director Lex Salisbury. During their investigation of this escape, authorities uncovered numerous questionable actions by Salisbury, who then resigned from the Zoo.

One of the most successful of the Zoo's projects, however, was the David A. Straz, Jr. Manatee Critical Care Center, opened in 1991 as part of the Sykes Florida Wildlife Center. The Straz Center is a full-on animal hospital that is specifically set up for the care of rescued native Manatees. Also sometimes known as the "sea cow", the Manatee's calm slow manner, big oven-mitt flippers, gentle black eyes, and roly-poly body, give them enormous "hug-appeal" to adults and kids alike. They are one of the favorites for Zoo-goers.

The West Indian Manatee (*Trichechus manatus*) is a large aquatic mammal that is native to the coastal areas of the Gulf of Mexico, the Caribbean and the northern parts of South America. (The Florida population is sometimes listed as a separate subspecies, *Trichechus manatus latirostris*.) West Indian Manatees can reach lengths of 10 feet and weigh as much as 1,200 pounds. There are three other members of the group Sirenidae—the West African Manatee (*Trichechus senegalensis*), the Amazon Manatee (*Trichechus inunguis*), and the more distantly related Dugong (*Dugong dugon*) from the Indian Ocean. A fifth species, the much-larger Steller's Sea Cow (*Hydrodamalis gigas*) once lived in the Bering Sea but was driven extinct by human hunters in the 1770's. All of the existing Sirenids are threatened or endangered in the wild.

In appearance, the Manatee is a large rotund animal with two flipper-like paddles in front and a large rounded flat tail in back. The gray wrinkled skin is bare except for a few coarse bristles and a dense mustache of whiskers on the upper lip. Their back is often encrusted with algae. They are totally aquatic and never leave the water. Although they can enter both fresh and salt water, they require warm temperatures and are limited to tropical areas where the water temperature seldom goes below 70 degrees. They are often found in estuaries, rivers, canals, and freshwater springs connected to the sea.

Despite being large and muscular, Manatees are very placid and slow-moving animals, paddling along slowly in search of the aquatic plants they graze on. They are very good swimmers, though, and often undertake long migrations. During warm summers they can sometimes be found in coastal areas as far north as Massachusetts. As mammals, they surface every so often to breathe, often just protruding their nose above the surface. They can hold their breath up to 20 minutes. Manatees eat up to 10% of their body weight a day in sea grasses and other aquatic plants.

The upper lip is elongated and prehensile, serving as a tool for the limbless animal to grasp plants. (The elongated upper lip also gives a clue to the Manatee's ancestry—the fossil record shows that the Sirenids evolved about 60 million years ago from four-footed wading mammals closely related to the Elephants.)

In many tests, Manatees have demonstrated a level of intelligence similar to Sea Lions or Dolphins.

Manatees, like most large mammals, have a very slow rate of reproduction, with just one calf every three or four years. They don't have a regular breeding season, though most calves are born in the spring. Pregnancy lasts for 12 months. At birth, the newborn Manatee is about 3.5 feet long and weighs about 50 pounds. Young Manatees stay with their mother for about two years before going off on their own, reaching sexual maturity at about five years old.

As Florida's human population grew in the 60's and 70's, the Manatees suffered devastating losses. Commercial and residential development of seashores and estuaries led to a huge loss in seagrass beds, one of the Manatee's primary food sources. Another widespread cause of death was collisions with motorboats—the slow-moving Manatees cannot get out of the way of a fast-moving boat. Even today, nearly every surviving Manatee you see will have a network of scars on its back caused by a speedboat propeller (field researchers use these scars to identify each individual Manatee).

To protect the species, the West Indian Manatee was included in the 1972 Marine Mammal Protection Act and was listed in the 1973 Endangered Species Act. In 1978, Florida passed its own Manatee Sanctuary Act. A massive effort was launched to restore the lost seagrass bed habitats, to establish "no wake" zones and manatee sanctuaries where motor boats are prohibited, and to educate boaters about protecting Manatees. It is estimated that there are about 5,000 Manatees now living in Florida.

The Manatee's cuddly appearance and gentle disposition have made them very popular with snorkelers and divers. Tourist areas like Crystal River have been built around Manatee habitat, especially warm-water areas like freshwater springs and power-plant lagoons where the Manatees tend to congregate in the winter. Although Federal and State laws prohibit approaching the Manatees, the inquisitive animals often will themselves approach the humans on their own, seeming to enjoy the interaction.

With its three 16,000 gallon "critical care tanks" and its two "recovery pools", the Straz Center was the first dedicated Manatee hospital in the US, and was formed in partnership with the University of Florida's College of Veterinary Medicine. In collaboration with the federal Fish and Wildlife Service and the state Fish and Wildlife Conservation Commission, volunteers from the Zoo rescue wild Manatees that have been stranded, orphaned or injured and bring them to the hospital for rehabilitation. Since 1991, the Center has rescued over 400 Manatees, with some 250 of these having been successfully returned to the wild.

104 *Lenny Flank*

HOUSTON ZOO
Houston, TX

Texas is a state that is proud of its history. Once a province of Mexico, Texans fought a long rebellion led by Sam Houston—culminating in the Alamo and the Battle of San Jacinto—to win its independence in 1836. That same year, the city of Houston was founded by two brothers named John and Augustus Allen. It became the capitol of what was then the independent Republic of Texas. By 1850 there were almost 3,000 residents.

Over the next several decades Texas would join the United States, then secede as part of the Confederacy before rejoining the US again. By 1870, Houston's population climbed to 10,000. Within twenty years, it was one of the most important port cities in the US.

Houston's first public park was established in August 1899 by Mayor Sam Brashear, who paid $26,000 for 4 acres of land. It was known as Sam Houston Park. Plans followed which envisioned expanding the parks system. In 1914, George Hermann, a member of the Parks Commission, donated 285 acres of his own land to the city, and the next year Mayor Ben Campbell approved purchase of another 122 acres by the Commission. A large tract of land was then set aside as Hermann Park, and additional land was purchased here in

1922 for a golf course, increasing the size of the park to 134 acres. Later, the city would add the Miller Outdoor Theatre and the Houston Museum of Natural Science.

Hermann Park had now become the city's centerpiece, so when it was decided to build a Zoo, the Park was the logical place for it, and a 55-acre expanse was set aside. The Houston Zoo opened in September 1922.

Hermann Park and the Houston Zoo quickly became popular with tourists and locals alike, and was soon receiving over a million guests a year. However, the city's commitment soon lagged far behind the continually-rising visitorship, and by 1980 both the Park and the Zoo were declining as the city's funding steadily fell.

In response, local citizens formed the Friends of Hermann Park (FHP), a nonprofit group, to lobby the city for increased funds to improve the Park. In 1997 the City Council approved a master plan, largely drawn up by FHP (which soon changed its name to the Hermann Park Conservancy), to renovate the area and renovating its walkways and reflecting pool.

The Houston Zoo was also targeted for improvement. In 2002, the City Council turned management of the facility over to the nonprofit Houston Zoo Inc, and funding was provided for an ambitious expansion, refurbishing many of the existing exhibits and adding several more.

The Houston Zoo has the second-highest visitorship of any Zoo in the US. One of the most popular areas is the Children's Zoo, which provides live interaction with animals from North America, South America, Asia and Africa, including Llamas, Goats, Ferrets and Sheep. There are also Prairie Dogs, Bats, and Raccoons on display. In addition, there is a Nursery for newborn Zoo animals.

The Bird House contains over 200 species, making it one of the largest bird collections in the world. Some of these are housed in glass displays, but many of them fly free in a large indoors open-air aviary with naturalistic trees and waterfalls.

The African Forest section displays animals from Africa, including Zebras, Rhinos, Giraffes, Red River Hogs, and Ostriches. The Chimpanzee and Lowland Gorilla colonies are housed in free-range paddocks, and the Gorilla habitat is designed to allow scientific study and observation. Nearby is the World of Primates, a boardwalk that winds through outdoors enclosures containing lemurs, monkeys, gibbons and Orangutans.

Other exhibit areas include the Asian Elephant Habitat, the South American Pantanel exhibit, the Reptile and Bug Houses, the Texas Wetlands display of native species, and the Natural Encounters area with small mammals.

The Zoo also participates in over a dozen conservation efforts, captive breeding programs, SSPs and assurance collection efforts. These center around species including Orangutans, Clouded Leopards, Okapi, Galapagos Tortoise, and African Painted Dogs.

The African Painted Dog (*Lycaon pictus*) historically ranged throughout sub-Saharan Africa, from Ethiopia all the way to South Africa. There are five recognized geographical subspecies, though this has been disputed. It is the largest dog in Africa.

This animal has long been known under a variety of names, including African Wild Dog, Cape Wild Dog, and Painted Wolf. Recently, several international conservation groups have begun emphasizing the name "Painted Dog" as an intentional effort to rehabilitate the species' undeserved reputation in Africa as a killer of livestock and sometimes of humans.

Although the Painted Dog is a member of the dog family, it is only distantly related to the other canids and is placed in a genus of its own, separated from other dogs by its lack of a dew claw and by some differences in the teeth. When it was first scientifically described back in 1820, the Painted Dog was mistakenly attributed as a Hyena, which it somewhat resembles in appearance. The spotted multicolor coat of the Painted Dog is unique for each animal, allowing individuals to be identified in the wild from photographs.

Like most dogs, the African Painted Dog lives and hunts in packs, and catches its prey by cooperatively running down injured or sick animals and killing them. The thin body build and long legs make them efficient runners, capable of pursuing speedier prey (often in relays) for long distances and eventually wearing it out. As highly intelligent pack hunters,

Painted Dogs have one of the highest effective kill rates of any other hunter, successfully making a kill in over 70% of their attempts. However, the Dogs also lose a substantial number of their kills to larger predators like Hyenas or Lions which can drive them away and take the dead prey for themselves.

When an individual dog spots potential prey, it will signal the others by "sneezing"—a short sharp exhalation through the nose. If other pack members are willing to join the hunt, they "sneeze" too, and once a sufficient number of hunters have "voted", they form a hunting group. The pack is led by a dominant pair of a female and her mate, and if they are one of the individuals who vote for a hunt, it's more likely for others to join in. A pack's typical hunting range can exceed 800 square miles.

Only the dominant pair in the pack is allowed to mate, and they produce a large litter of around ten pups. The pups are protected inside a den and fed with regurgitated meat until they are mobile enough to join the pack. Painted Dogs have no real predators of their own, but larger predators like Lions and Hyenas will often kill them to remove potential competition. New packs are formed when a subordinate female leaves the pack to find a mate elsewhere.

But the wild populations of African Painted Dogs are steadily declining. By the 1950s, their estimated numbers were around 500,000. By 2020, they had decreased to roughly 6,000 in the wild and had been eliminated from most of their range, remaining only in southern and eastern Africa. This is due mostly to habitat loss as savannah and grasslands continue to be converted into human settlements. Painted Dogs are also viewed, inaccurately, as threats to domestic Cattle, Goats and Sheep, and they are routinely shot by ranchers and pastoral herders.

Today, African Painted Dogs are protected by a number of national parks in Botswana, Kenya, Mozambique, Namibia, South Africa, Tanzania, Zambia, and Zimbabwe. Small packs are kept and exhibited in several Zoos worldwide, mostly as an assurance colony.

But there are also captive breeding programs, and the Houston Zoo has been an active participant for several years. One of the Zoo's male Painted Dogs, named Ghost, was sent to

Binder Park Zoo in Michigan on a breeding loan, and four of the puppies he produced, named Modo, Rafiki, Tamu and Wiki, were returned to Houston in 2020. In 2016, three females were imported from a Zoo in England and introduced to two of the Houston Zoo's males, Mikita and Blaze, to form a new breeding pack. As with all captive-breeding programs, these pairings are carefully calculated as part of the Species Survival Plan to produce the maximum possible genetic divergence in the population.

By the 2010s, the Houston Zoo was planning another ambitious expansion under a new $72 million master plan. Future projects included remodeling and updating some of the existing exhibits, and adding a series of new ones to include Arctic World, Tropical World, Desert World, Invisible World, Island World, and an Aquarium.

Plans were also being made for a 24,000-acre tract of land near Addicks Dam called Cullen Park, which had been leased from the Army Corps of Engineers in the 1980s. New planned improvements there included a display of Texas cattle breeds, and a "living history" replica farmstead from the 1890s.

Another 1,000 acres of the new park were set aside for a planned Zoo facility to be known as the Cullen Park Zoo. Part of this will be public exhibits, and the rest will be devoted to veterinary facilities and large open-air enclosures for housing hoofed herd animals, Elephants, and wide-ranging carnivores (like Painted Dogs) for captive breeding.

DENVER ZOO
Denver CO

In 1896, an admirer presented the Mayor of Denver, Thomas McMurry, with an unusual gift. This was an orphaned Black Bear cub that had been named Billy Bryan, after the perennial Presidential candidate William Jennings Bryan. McMurray turned the cub over to the City Park. Here, a cage was constructed for Billy and he was put on public display.

The City Park Zoo's collection expanded, mostly from gifts and donations of local native species. There was a flock of Ducks, a herd of Bison, a town of Prairie Dogs, a Wolf pack, and a group of Elk. Somebody contributed a colony of Rhesus Monkeys, and someone else added a number of Chinese Pheasants—several of which escaped, became established in the wild, and over time populated much of the state. When some of the Red Squirrels also escaped and began taking over the park, the city made plans to shoot them, but this provoked outraged cries from local animal lovers, and they were trapped instead and relocated to other parks.

By 1906, the City Park Zoo had grown to a size where it needed to become more organized, and Mayor Robert Speer (who had campaigned with a "City Beautiful" slogan) hired Victor Borcherdt as Zoo Director. Working with city landscape architect Saco DeBoer, they set out to design a new Zoo.

Influenced by Carl Hagenbeck's revolutionary work in Europe with free-roaming animals in naturalistic open spaces, the Denver Zoo became one of the first in the United States to bring the idea here.

The centerpiece of the new Zoo was Bear Mountain. This large enclosure was surrounded by a pedestrian walking path and a deep hidden dry moat. Inside were native trees, rocks, caves, and an artificial river. To make a simulated mountainside, workers took plaster casts from a real nearby cliff and molded it in cement that was dyed in various shades to look like real layered sedimentary rock. The enclosure was divided into three sections. At the tip was a smaller space for the Rhesus Monkeys (they proved to be too adept at escapes, however, and were soon replaced with California Sea Lions). The rest of the area was split in two, with Polar Bears on one side and Grizzly Bears on the other. The whole project cost $50,000—an enormous sum at the time.

When the Bear Mountain exhibit opened in 1918, it was an instant hit, and other Zoos across the country sent people to study it and adapt Hagenbeck's concept for their own enclosures. One newspaper noted that the display was "something of an experiment, but it was so immediately and entirely successful that it became the envy of other cities." During the Great Depression, the Denver Zoo used Federal money and workers from the WPA to open another moated artificial mountain—Monkey Island, which opened in 1937.

There then, unfortunately, followed a decade of neglect. The Zoo's budget declined, upkeep and maintenance suffered, and many of the displays fell into disrepair. When new Mayor Quigg Newton took office in 1947, he made it a priority to revitalize and update the Zoo.

Newton hired architect Saco DeBoer—the same person who had helped produce the original design forty years before—and drew up a new program to expand the Zoo. The first step was to encourage public support and participation, and in 1950 a community fundraising drive was launched to purchase the Zoo's first Elephant, named Cookie. She was temporarily housed in the city's water pumping station before her new paddock was finished. Cookie was joined by another Elephant, named Candy, in 1959.

Next, the city established the Denver Zoological Foundation, a nonprofit citizen's group which formally took over management of the Zoo in 1956. The Foundation drew up an ambitious Master Plan to greatly expand the facilities over a period of 25 years.

The first project to be completed was the Feline House in 1961 (which was, many years later, converted to Stingray Cove). This was followed in 1975 by Bird World, a large indoors free-flight aviary, and then twelve years after that by the Northern Shore exhibit, which relocated the Sea Lions and Polar Bears from the newly refurbished Bear Mountain. The final part of the 1959 Master Plan was the $11 million Tropical Discovery, which opened in 1993 and featured reef fish, reptiles, amphibians, and jungle spiders and insects.

In 1995 a new Master Plan was produced which focused heavily on conservation and education efforts. The first new exhibit under the Millenium Master Plan was the 7-acre Primate Panorama, followed by Predator Ridge, a display of African savannah predators which introduced the concept of "rotating exhibits", where animals were moved periodically from one enclosure to another as an enrichment experience. A new and expanded Elephant paddock was added to the Zoo in 2012.

The Zoo also began to work with a number of different species as part of its captive breeding and conservation programs. It was the first Zoo in North America to breed the Aye-Aye, a lemur from Madagascar. There were also successful programs with Lake Titicaca Frogs, Boreal Toads, and Indian Rhino. And another of the Zoo's programs has focused on Przewalski's Horse.

When Genghis Khan and his Mongols swept across Asia and Europe in the Middle Ages and established one of the largest empires ever seen, they were riding stocky short-limbed horses that had evolved in the grassy steppes, quite different to the Arabian horses that had always been known in Europe. The source of these Mongolian steeds was virtually unknown to the rest of the world, however, until 1881, when a Russian Army mapmaker named Nikolai Przewalski, who was exploring in remote Mongolia, managed to obtain the skull and skin of an unusually small and stocky horse he found living there, called "Takhi" by the natives, and sent it to a scientific institute in St Petersburg. They gave it the scientific name *Equus przewalskii*, but the taxonomic status of Przewalski's Horse is still disputed, with some authorities considering it as a subspecies of the Eurasian Wild Horse *Equus ferus*, while others class it as just another variety of the domestic horse subspecies *Equus ferus caballus*. Genetic analysis indicates that Przewalski's Horse may be a feral variety of the domesticated horses from the ancient Botai tribe in central Asia, though this is also disputed.

In any case, everyone agrees about two things: Przewalski's Horse is distinctly different from any other horse, and it is one of the most seriously endangered animals in the world.

At one time, the steppe grassland habitat stretched across Europe and much of Asia, and Cro-Magnon cave paintings depict similar wild horses living in France 30,000 years ago. But as the Ice Age ended, Europe became covered with forest and the grassland horses were pushed further east into central Asia.

Przewalski's Horse was confined to portions of China, Mongolia and Kazakhstan. Here they lived in two distinct types of herds. The females and their young lived together under the watchful eye of a dominant stallion, who monopolized breeding with all the mares in the herd. Young male horses lived separately in bachelor herds, where they remained until they were mature enough to successfully challenge a dominant stallion and win control of his herd of mares.

Unfortunately for the horses, the grassland habitat that they needed was also favored by human farmers, and the surviving remnants of Przewalski's Horse herds were pushed into smaller and smaller areas as their grazing lands were converted into farmsteads. By the time Przewalski had sent his specimens to St Petersburg, the wild steppe horses were already extremely rare: Przewalski had in fact been specifically looking for them, based on some stories he heard about them.

After Przewalski's report, Zoos around the world sent expeditions to capture some of the rare horses for display. This turned out to be fortunate, since the wild populations declined rapidly. By the 1940s the Horses could be readily found only in the harsh area of the Gobi Desert. One of the last herds, in a remote part of the Soviet Ukraine, was shot and eaten by occupying German soldiers during World War II. At the end of the war the Przewalski's Horses in American Zoos had all died out and there were only two captive groups remaining, in Munich and Prague.

Once it was realized how rapidly the wild Horse was declining, several Zoos around the world sent expeditions to Mongolia to obtain specimens, but only a few were ever found. The last known herd was gone by 1967, and no Przewalski's Horse was seen anywhere after 1969. The species was declared extinct in the wild. All that remained was the tiny number of animals that still survived in Zoos.

In a desperate attempt to save the species from total extinction, two Dutch researchers started the Foundation for the Preservation and Protection of the Przewalski Horse in 1977. The Foundation drew up a detailed plan to breed the various individuals being held in Zoos in a way that would maximize their genetic diversity and help minimize inbreeding. It became the model for the modern Species Survival Plan. In the end, only fourteen animals were successfully mated, and every Przewalski's Horse in the world today is descended from those fourteen individuals.

Since then, Przewalski's Horse has been the focus of an intense program of captive breeding. There are a number of centers which breed the horses in a naturalistic setting and prepare them for release into the wild: one of these is at Askania Nova Preserve in Ukraine, and another is at Le Villaret in France's Cevennes National Park. Individual horses have been spread to a number of Zoos around the world as an assurance collection, and these are regularly moved around for selective breeding.

In the wild, a number of preserves and parks have been established to provide protected areas where captive-bred herds can be re-established in the wild. These include Khustain Nuruu National Park, the Takhi Kal Preserve, and Khar Us Nuur National Park—all in Mongolia—and Kalamely Mountain Preserve in China. In the Ukraine, a park has been established at Askania Nova. After the Chernobyl nuclear accident, an "Exclusion Zone" was established around the destroyed nuclear reactor which became an unintentional wildlife refuge, and in 1998 a herd of several dozen captive-bred Przewalski's Horses was introduced there. They grew to over 100 individuals, but were later reduced by poaching in the wake of the collapse of the Russian economy.

The Denver Zoo, along with the Smithsonian National Zoo, the San Diego Zoo, the Prague Zoo in the Czech Republic, the Xinjiang Wild Horse Breeding Centre in China, and the Taronga Western Plains Zoo in Australia, have all had effective captive-breeding herds, and have successfully introduced individuals into these wild populations. By 2020, it was estimated that there were about 2000 Przewalski's Horses in existence, and around 300 of these were free-roaming in the wild.

CINCINNATI ZOO
Cincinnati OH

In 1854, the prominent French biologist Isidore Geoffroy Saint-Hilaire helped organize a group in Paris that called itself the "Society for Acclimatization", which had as its stated goal the introduction and establishment of plants and animals into France from around the world, "such as may be useful or desirable". Within a few years, similar societies appeared around the world. They were particularly popular in colonial regions, where homesick Europeans embraced the idea of bringing in familiar plants and animals to make them feel more at home. While the idea of deliberately bringing in non-native wildlife may strike us today as odd or even dangerous, the practice reflected the political and social ideas of the time that European culture (in all its aspects) was superior to the wild savagery of the rest of the world and that it was a service to humanity to bring "Europe" everywhere.

"Acclimatization Societies" appeared across the world, from England to Australia, and in 1872 they reached Ohio. The Society for the Acclimatization of Birds, in Cincinnati, began importing several different species of birds from Europe. The ostensible purpose was to bring in insect-eating birds to help control an outbreak of caterpillars, but one suspects that, in a nation of immigrants, many people just wanted to have a familiar bit of home.

Some of the birds that Acclimatization Societies brought in turned out to be serious mistakes: America owes its invasive Starlings and English Sparrows to these rather misguided efforts. But we can also thank the Society in Cincinnati for the Zoo: as the birds arrived—hundreds of them—Society members had to house them, feed them and care for them until they could be released in a good spot. And that planted the idea of having a zoological garden in the city.

Along with other citizens, members of the Acclimatization Society formed the nonprofit Zoological Society of Cincinnati and in 1874 obtained a lease from the city for a 64-acre tract of land in what was then known as Blakely Woods. When the Zoo opened in September 1875, most of the exhibits were birds that had been brought in by the Acclimatization Society, but there was also a smattering of other animals that had been obtained through various means, including eight monkeys, six Raccoons, three White-Tail Deer, two Caribou, two Grizzly Bears, a Bison, a Hyena, a Tiger, an Alligator, and an Asian Elephant that had been bought from a traveling circus. The original Primate House (which was later remodeled into the Reptile House) is today the oldest existing Zoo building in the US and is, along with the Elephant House, registered as a National Historic Landmark.

At this time the Cincinnati area was heavily populated by immigrants, most of whom still spoke German (the Zoo's first English-language guidebook wasn't printed until 17 years later). Although the local business community supported the Zoo, it struggled financially. In its first ten years the Zoological Society had to sell off 22 acres of land to avoid falling into debt, and by 1898 it was virtually bankrupt. The whole operation was purchased by the Cincinnati Zoological Company, a for-profit group of local businessmen, but they couldn't meet expenses either, and the Zoo passed over to the Cincinnati Traction Company, a trolley line which ran it as a promotional tool. In 1917 another nonprofit society, the Cincinnati Zoological Park Association, took over and managed to raise money from the local business community to keep the Zoo open. It wasn't until 1932 that the Zoo finally became financially stable, when it was bought by the City and run by the Parks Department.

Finally with a steady budget, the Zoo began a process of renovation and expansion. The open-air African Veldt exhibit was opened in 1935 and would remain the largest area in the Zoo for several decades. The Zoo would go on to add more exhibits, including the Red Panda Habitat, the Elephant Reserve, Gorilla World, Cat Canyon, Manatee Springs, and a refurbished Children's Zoo. By 2020 there were around 2,000 animals from 500 different species on exhibit. The Zoo is also involved with a large number of Species Survival Plans, research projects, and educational programs (as a partner with the Cincinnati Public School System), administered by the Lindner Center for Conservation and Research of Endangered Wildlife.

Sadly, though, the Cincinnati Zoo is probably most famous as the site where the last stage of an extinction took place—one that helped spark the modern conservation movement.

In 1491, the Passenger Pigeon (*Ectopistes migratorius*), may have been the most abundant bird species on Earth. Living in flocks that contained as many as two billion individual birds, it has been estimated that this single species made up some 40% of all the birds in North America. Flocks of Passenger Pigeons could stretch literally from horizon to horizon; some flocks were over 100 miles long. There are contemporary reports of flocks shading out the sun for hours as they flew overhead in an unending stream (leading to the bird's name, from the French *passager*—"to pass by").

And yet, on September 1, 1914, the very last existing Passenger Pigeon, a 29-year resident at the Cincinnati Zoo named "Martha", died in her cage of old age, marking the extinction of what had been one of the most abundant animals on Earth.

The Passenger Pigeon was a member of the Columbidae family of birds, which includes the pigeons and doves. Genetic analysis has shown that its closest relative is the Band-Tailed Pigeon from the American West. Fossil finds have shown that the bird had been living in North America for at least 100,000 years, and once stretched all the way to California. In appearance, it was a bit bigger than a modern Mourning Dove, with a slate-gray back and a reddish belly, with the males having brighter and more iridescent colors.

The birds lived in the dense temperate forests of eastern North America, feeding primarily on acorns, insects, chestnuts, and beechnuts. They were highly gregarious and social, and colonies often covered many square miles with millions of birds. During the spring breeding season, hundreds of nests would appear in each tree, where mated females laid a single egg, and both parents fed and cared for the hatchling. Just before the young bird was ready to fledge, the parents would abandon it, and the nestling would flutter down to the ground and fend for itself, feeding on worms, seeds and insects until they were big enough to fly. During this period they were easy prey for predators, but because there were tens of thousands of hatchling birds, the predators were swamped by sheer numbers, and most of the young birds survived.

Such an easy food source was not neglected, and Native American tribes in the eastern US made many a meal out of Passenger Pigeons—as did the European settlers when they colonized the continent in the 18th and 19th centuries. The birds were so numerous that the humans barely made a dent in the population.

But technology would change that. By the 1850's, the US was no longer a farming society—it was becoming urban and industrial. Over the years, farmland gave way to cities and towns; railroads networked the entire country. Much of the dense eastern woodlands that provided habitat for the birds was disappearing; by 1900, most of the original forests in the eastern half of the US were gone.

As the birds became concentrated into smaller and smaller remaining patches of habitat, they became easier to hunt. Meanwhile, railroads made it easier to transport huge numbers of killed birds to market, and refrigeration technology allowed them to reach every table. Instead of the individual subsistence hunting that humans had been carrying out for thousands of years, now the birds were systematically exterminated on an industrial scale, and their enormously-successful survival tactic—living in huge groups that swamped and overwhelmed predators—became one of the instruments of their doom.

Professional pigeon hunters began following the flocks by railroad, and tens of millions of birds were being shipped each year to feed the big cities on the coast, where they sold for 3 or 4 cents each. Their feathers were also used as a substitute for duck or goose in pillows or comforters. Many frontier towns depended almost solely on the Passenger Pigeon both for income and for its own food supply. The birds were easiest to catch as "squab" groundlings during the nesting season, but they could also be taken by setting a nesting tree on fire and picking up the roasted or escaping individuals. And special nets were designed that could be placed in front of flocks to capture hundreds of birds at a time.

The combined effect of habitat loss and hunting at this massive scale was too much for the pigeons. Their breeding cycle was affected as well: the pigeons would only breed when they were present in large contiguous flocks, not in individual pairs. Because of this, efforts by Zoos and conservationists to breed the species all failed.

By the 1890's, the species had declined severely. Large flocks became harder and harder to find. States began passing laws restricting or even banning pigeon hunting. Most of these were ignored. The rapid disappearance of the pigeons also led to Federal action. In 1900 the Lacey Act was passed, which prohibited the interstate sale of illegally-collected birds.

But it came too late for the Passenger Pigeon. In March of that same year, a boy with a BB gun killed the last known wild Passenger Pigeon, in Ohio. After that, the species existed only as scattered groups in Zoos, which refused to breed. On September 1, 1914, the last of these Zoo pigeons, Martha, died in Cincinnati. She had never laid a fertile egg. What had once been the most common bird in America was now extinct.

All that remains of the Passenger Pigeon today are a handful of preserved eggshells and some taxidermy mounts. Martha's body was frozen, skinned, mounted, and sent to the Smithsonian Institution, where she is part of the research collection.

Today, there are occasional plans floated to extract DNA from the remaining taxidermy mounts and use it to clone the species back into existence (an idea that is also sometimes suggested for other extinct species ranging from Thylacine

Wolves to Woolly Mammoths). But without the extensive forested woodland habitat and the huge social flocks that the Passenger Pigeon needed to survive and breed, the species would never be able to return to the wild, and would exist only as living museum pieces.

At the Cincinnati Zoo, Martha is commemorated by a memorial statue and a stone building where her cage used to be. Built in 1915, the display tells the story of the Passenger Pigeon. The structure is listed as a National Historic Landmark.

In 2018, the Zoo was planning another round of expansion and renovation, under the catchphrase "More Home to Roam". Plans called for $150 million in improvements and new exhibits. Most of the work had been completed by 2020.

PITTSBURGH ZOO
Pittsburgh PA

By the 1890s, the United States, which had been a largely agricultural society, was transformed into a rapidly-expanding industrial powerhouse, with factories and mills sprouting up in every urban area. The steel industry was the core of the American economy, and the city of Pittsburgh was the heart of the steel industry. It was a place of robber barons like Andrew Carnegie and Henry Frick, and of violent industrial warfare like the Homestead strike.

Christopher Magee wanted to help soften the city's steely-cold image. The owner of the Fort Pitt Traction trolley company, Magee was also the publisher of one of Pittsburgh's newspapers and had served as a Pennsylvania State Senator. On Christmas Eve 1895, Magee wrote to the city government with a proposal. Declaring, "No more interesting or instructive institutions can be found in the great cities of the world than the Zoological Gardens," and pointing out that other cities like New York, Cincinnati, and Philadelphia already had public Zoos, Magee offered $125,000 (over $4 million in 2020 dollars) to finance the construction of a Zoo in Pittsburgh's Highland Park if the city would donate the land for it and assume the cost of running it.

It was an offer that was too good to pass up, and the Pittsburgh Zoo opened in July 1898. Many of the animals, including Gusky the Elephant, were relocated from a menagerie that had been set up in Schenley Park. The new Zoo consisted of a crescent-shaped building with two octagonal towers at each end. Like all Zoos of the time, the 300 or so animals were housed in stark iron-bar cement cages. But the public loved it: nearly 10,000 guests visited on opening day.

Unfortunately the city fudged on its side of the bargain. Funding was skimpy, and by the time of the stock market crash in 1929 the Pittsburgh Zoo was in poor shape. In 1937 the Works Progress Administration (WPA), one of Franklin Roosevelt's New Deal programs, stepped in with funding and manpower, and a project was undertaken to modernize the Zoo. By this time, the old notions of cement prison-cell cages were being replaced with Carl Hagenbeck's vision of roomy outdoors pens, and, embracing this concept, the new Bear exhibits, built in three sections, contained naturalistic settings with trees and rocks, surrounded by a dry moat and low wall. There were Black Bears from Pennsylvania, a Kodiak Bear from Alaska, and Spectacled Bears from South America. Twelve years later, a grant from the Sarah Mellon Scaife Foundation, funded by the city's prominent banking family, led to a Children's Zoo, which has been remodeled several times since then and renamed Kid's Kingdom. It contains a petting zoo, Sea Lions, and some native Pennsylvania species like White-Tail Deer and Beavers.

In 1967, the Zoo took a new direction when it opened AquaZoo, a full-fledged aquarium exhibit. At the time, it was the only public Aquarium in Pennsylvania and one of only a handful of Zoos worldwide with an attached Aquarium display. AquaZoo was updated and expanded in 2000, re-emerging as the $17 million two-story PPG Aquarium, with reef fish, penguins, Amazon River life, and native Pennsylvania fishes, otters, turtles, and other aquatic life.

The Pittsburgh Zoo's largest expansion came in the 80s, when all of the remaining animal pens were either remodeled or replaced. The Asian Forest (later renamed Forest Passage) and the African Forest areas opened within four years of each other, and were followed by the five-acre Tropical Forest indoors enclosure for the primates. They contain a variety of species including Amur Leopards, Red Pandas, Cheetahs, Lemurs, and Nyala. In 1992 a new building was opened for the reptiles and small mammals. One of the animals here was "Otis", a ten-foot American Alligator who was illegally taken from the wild in Florida as a youngster and brought back to Pennsylvania by a vacationing family, before he was confiscated by state wildlife authorities and turned over to the Zoo.

The Zoo's management also changed. In 1994, the operation was turned over to the nonprofit Zoological Society of Pittsburgh, which expanded the educational and conservation programs. A new building housed classrooms, a lecture hall and a research library. New exhibits followed: The Islands opened in 2015 and featured island species like Siamangs and Warty Pigs, and Jungle Odyssey, with Ocelots, Capybaras and Pygmy Hippos, came two years after that.

The Zoo has had many breeding successes, including African Elephants, Amur Tigers, Sea Lions and African Painted Dogs. The Zoo has also produced several litters of captive-bred Canada Lynx kittens.

There are four species of Lynx which range across most of the northern hemisphere. The Eurasian Lynx is found from Europe to Siberia, and the Iberian Lynx is limited to the west of Europe. In North America, the Canada Lynx (*Lynx canadensis*) ranges across Alaska and Canada and into the northernmost continental US; further south it is replaced by its smaller cousin the Bobcat. The Canada Lynx used to be divided into several subspecies, but DNA sequencing has shown that there is virtually no real genetic difference between them. Fossils indicate that the Lynx originally evolved in Asia and crossed the Beringia land bridge into North America about 8 million years ago.

The Lynx is specialized for a life in the snowy forests of the boreal north. The fur is thick and dense to provide warmth, the paws are extra-wide to act as snowshoes, and the tail is short to prevent freezing. A medium-sized cat, weighing around 35 pounds, the Lynx is powerfully muscled to allow it to plow its way through deep snow.

The Canada Lynx is, however, only about half the size of its Eurasian cousin. It is therefore adapted to smaller prey, and feeds almost exclusively on the Snowshoe Hare, which it hunts by ambush along pathways and trails. Lynx will also capture squirrels, ducks, moles and grouse, and if desperate they are capable of killing deer fawns and even young Caribou. Although the cats are good swimmers and also adept at climbing trees, they hunt only on the ground, usually at night. Because they are so heavily dependent upon Snowshoe Hare populations, Lynx are widely studied by ecologists as a mathematical model for understanding predator-prey relationships.

Females can range over as much as 50 square miles, while a male's territory is usually twice as large. The cats are mostly solitary unless mating, though there are occasional reports of a pair hunting together. Breeding season is in the spring when food is available, and the litter size varies according to the amount of ready food. The kittens go off on their own at a year old, though they don't reach full maturity for another year after that.

In the wild Lynx may live for 10-15 years. Although young Lynx are occasionally caught and eaten by Martens, and Coyotes can also be a danger (as well as a competitor for food), the population levels of wild Lynx seem to be strongly determined by the cyclical ups and downs of the Snowshoe Hare population. Lynx have long been trapped by humans for their luxurious thick fur, however, and even today the number of pelts taken from the wild can range from 15,000 to 7,000 a year.

In the northern Canadian parts of its range, the cat's population seems to be stable, and the IUCN lists the Lynx as a "Species of Least Concern". But in southern Canada and in those US states where the Lynx has historically been found, local populations are much lower (and the cats are entirely absent from much of their former range). The United States has listed the species as "Threatened".

In 1989, state wildlife officials in New York, where the cats have been absent for many years and are considered "extinct", attempted to reintroduce Lynx back into the wild by relocating 80 individuals that had been captured in northern Canada.

However, the attempt failed: many of the Lynx were hit by cars, and others were mistakenly shot by Bobcat hunters. Some of the cats moved into neighboring states which apparently had better habitat. Ten years later, another attempt at reintroduction was made, this time in Colorado. By 2010 these Lynx were successfully breeding in the wild in the San Juan Mountains and had spread through Summit County.

Only about 2% of the total Lynx population reaches the US, however, and these are concentrated in Maine, Minnesota, Montana, Idaho and Washington. Though these populations are thin, studies seem to show that they are stable and perhaps increasing. This may lead to the removal of the Lynx from the "Threatened Species" list.

The Pittsburgh Zoo obtained a female Canada Lynx from the New York State Zoo in January 2017, after its Snow Leopard died of cancer, and she is mated each year with a male from other Zoos that has been selected for genetic variability. Pittsburgh produced its first litter, of five kittens, in 2018. Another four kittens arrived in 2019, which were named Bjorn, Ragnar, Helga and Lagertha.

OKLAHOMA CITY ZOO
Oklahoma City OK

The Oklahoma City Zoo was founded before the State of Oklahoma was. In 1902, when Oklahoma was still a US Territory consisting mostly of Native American reservations, someone donated a Deer to Wheeler Park in Oklahoma City. It's not known where or how they got it, but a Deer was a pretty rare thing out on the plains, and lots of people stopped at the Park to look at it. Soon others began to drop off animals they had caught: Bears, Wolves, and Eagles. Within a year there were several dozen animals housed in makeshift pens at the park, and in September 1903 the City officially christened it Wheeler Park Zoo, billing it as "The First Zoo in the Southwest". It stood for the next twenty years, visited by Easterners who had moved West to seek a new life but who seldom ventured out into the actual wilderness. For most of them, the animal life of the Great Plains was as exotic as anything from the Amazon or Congo.

Then it all got swept away. In 1923, the Great Flood hit Oklahoma City, washing away many of the town's homes and businesses. It also washed away most of the Zoo. The surviving animals were gathered up at the Fairgrounds and were kept there until the City could purchase a tract of land to put them. This became Lincoln Park, and in 1925 the Zoo officially moved there.

Just a few years later, the West endured the twin curses of the Dust Bowl and the Great Depression. But for the Lincoln Park Zoo, the hardship turned out to be a blessing. One of the New Deal programs launched by President Franklin Roosevelt was the Works Progress Administration, which had the job of carrying out public-works projects as a way of getting Americans back to work. The WPA set aside over $200,000 to pay for a major facelift for the little Zoo.

The work was extensive. Workers from the Civilian Conservation Corp Camp 895 replaced most of the fences with large paddocks enclosed by sturdy stone walls, which allowed for large animals like Elephants and Bears. At Monkey Island, an entire wooden ship was placed inside the sunken stone enclosure, where a colony of 35 Rhesus Monkeys and 5 Ring-Tailed Lemurs were free to scramble around the towering masts. (The Lemurs were later removed after they began bullying all the Monkeys.)

A number of buildings were constructed both for the animals and for use as Zoo offices and storage. An outdoor amphitheater with seating for 1,000 people was intended for concerts, theater, speeches, and the occasional circus acts. By the time the Zoo held its official re-dedication service in 1938, it had been transformed from a simple parkside menagerie into one of the most modern Zoos in the country. Many of the WPA-era projects are still in use today.

The new Lincoln Park Zoo (which would be officially renamed the Oklahoma City Zoo in 2001) was instantly popular with local citizens—perhaps helped by the fact that there was no admission charge. When the Zoo obtained its first Elephant, named Judy, she was paid for by donations raised by the city's schoolchildren.

As the Zoo continued to grow, it expanded. In the 1950s a new Primate House was built for the monkeys and great apes; it was replaced in 1993 by a larger open-air exhibit called Great EscApe. The old Monkey Island was torn down in 1998 and was replaced with a new entrance plaza. One of the grottoes held Dolphins from 1986 till 2001, when they were replaced by a colony of California Sea Lions. Fittingly, the

Zoozeum, a collection of documents and photos from the Zoo's history, is housed in one of the buildings that had been constructed by the WPA back in 1935.

In 1962, an odd tragedy occurred. Then-Director Warren Thomas, who had already delivered the first captive-born Gorilla at the Columbus Zoo and would later go on to run the Los Angeles Zoo, had been convinced by researcher Dr. Jolyon West to try an experiment that involved dosing an Elephant with the hallucinogenic drug LSD. Obligingly, Thomas shot a hypodermic needle containing a whopping dosage into Tusko, one of the Zoo's Asian Elephants. Tusko staggered around for about 90 minutes, collapsed, and died.

Today the Oklahoma City Zoo covers about 100 acres. There is a ten-acre Expedition Asia section, a Children's Zoo, and an indoors Aquarium called Aquaticus. Oklahoma Trails exhibits native wildlife, while the Cat Forest displays a variety of felines from all over the world. There is also a Butterfly Garden, a Tram, Swan Boats, a Carousel, a Playground, the Island Life Herpetarium, and a Choo Choo Train. The Zoo receives about one million visitors per year.

Despite its relatively small size and budget, the Oklahoma City Zoo participates in a number of different conservation and captive-breeding programs. One of these centers around the unusual Père David's Deer, which was saved from extinction only by the presence of a single captive herd in the Emperor of China's private garden.

In 1864, the French Catholic priest Father (*Père*, in French) Armand David was living near the Imperial Palace in Beijing as a missionary. A keen naturalist, he spent much of his spare time collecting and examining the local plants and wildlife, and would later become famous as the first Westerner to describe the Giant Panda. But he was intrigued by one particular story that he kept hearing from courtiers about an unusual deer called *Mi-lu* that, the story went, had "the hooves of a cow but not a cow, the neck of a camel but not a camel, antlers of a deer but not a deer, the tail of a donkey but not a donkey." In Chinese mythology, it was known as *Sibuxiang*, and it was the mythical mount of the great sage Jiang Ziya when he rode into battle against the tyrannical King Zhou of Shang. Nowadays, David was told, the fabled *Mi-lu* only existed in one place: the Nanyuan Imperial Hunting Park near the palace in Beijing. This was a large tract of land that, hundreds of years ago, had been completely enclosed by a high wall and stocked with game animals, including the *Mi-lu*, for the exclusive use of the Chinese Emperors.

David, intrigued by the story, asked to see the strange beast. But not only was the Hunting Park strictly off-limits to foreigners, but Chinese people were not allowed to go inside it either, or even to look in through the gate—under penalty of death. The entire park was guarded by a unit of Imperial troops.

And so, the Catholic priest resorted to a rather un-Christian expedient—one day as a section of the wall was being repaired, David bribed one of the guards to let him stand on a pile of bricks and look over the top. Just as he did, a herd of odd-looking deer passed by: they had long tails, flattish heads, large rounded feet, strange fanglike teeth, and unusual antlers with prongs facing the wrong way.

Immediately, David recognized that they were a new species that was unknown to science. A year later, with some more bribery, David was able to procure a pair of antlers and two hides, which he dispatched back to France. There they were examined by the naturalist Henri Milne-Edwards, who identified it as an unusual species of deer, so odd that he placed it in its own genus under the Latin name *Elaphurus davidianus*. In Father David's honor, it became known as Père David's Deer.

It turned out that the 34 Père David's Deer in Beijing were in fact the only ones in the world. Fossils were later found indicating that the unusual animal had once been widespread in southeastern China, where it lived in wet swampland. However, as ancient China's human population expanded and wetlands were turned into rice paddies and villages, the Père David's Deer lost its habitat and was now extinct in the wild, surviving only within the protection of the Emperor's private park since at least the time of the Yuan Dynasty in 1205, and perhaps as early as the 4th Century.

As soon as the rare new species was published in the scientific literature, every Zoo in Europe wanted one, and the Imperial Court in Beijing was inundated with requests for a gift of one of his Deer. Over the next few decades, some Zoos were given a specimen as a gesture of diplomatic goodwill by the Emperor, and some Deer were illegally smuggled out through bribery and pay-offs. By 1890 there were about 20 Père David's Deer in Europe.

It turned out to be a stroke of good fortune. In 1894 a flood on the nearby Han River broke open part of the wall surrounding the Nanyuan Hunting Park, and about half of the Deer inside escaped into the surrounding countryside—where they were killed and eaten by Chinese peasants. Then, in 1900, the Boxer Rebellion swept across China, and the rebels broke into the Hunting Park and ate the rest of the Deer. That left only a few individuals in the Beijing Zoo, which were dead by 1922. The Père David's Deer was now extinct in its native land.

There remained only the scattered individuals in Europe's Zoos, and they would each have died off eventually too, eliminating the entire species, had it not been for the British Duke of Bedford. Bedford purchased all 18 of the remaining Père David's Deer in Europe and gathered them together at his Woburn Abbey estate. The Deer adapted well to the rolling English countryside, and 11 of them successfully bred. Through World War One and World War Two, the herd expanded in fits and starts. In 1956, several individuals were sent from Woburn to the Beijing Zoo.

Financed largely through the private efforts of the Duke of Bedford and then his son, the population of Père David's Deer increased over the years, and to safeguard the herd the animals were distributed to four other wildlife parks in the UK. In 1985, a group of 5 males and 15 females was donated to China, followed by another group of 18 females in 1987. The Chinese Government established its breeding program at the old site of the Nanyuan Imperial Hunting Park, calling it Mi-lu Park. After almost 90 years, the Père David's Deer had returned home.

In 1997, a much larger reserve was established in a remote part of eastern China near the Yellow Sea that was called the Dafeng Mi-lu Nature Preserve, and captive-bred Père David's Deer from Mi-lu Park were released there in an attempt to establish a wild population. By 2005 there were almost 1000 Père David's Deer living in the Dafeng Preserve. Another group of wild Deer had been established at the Hubei Shishou Milu National Nature Reserve. In 1998, a severe flood led to the escape of part of the Hubei Shishou herd, which then successfully established itself in an area outside the Preserve. There are now at least 2000 Père David's Deer living either in various Preserves or in the wild.

As part of the captive breeding program, small herds have also been distributed to a number of Zoos around the world, where they are now on display as part of the public education and outreach effort. One of these locations is the Oklahoma City Zoo.

But a big question mark remains concerning the survival of the Père David's Deer in the wild. For perhaps 1000 years, these animals have been living in isolation, first in China and then in England, with human care and protection from their natural predators—Tigers and Leopards. In that time, they have become, in a sense, domesticated and adapted to living under the care of humans. In the Dafeng and Hubei Shishou Preserves in China, they live in areas that are mostly predator-free. The Deer here also receive supplemental food from humans.

Since the Père David's Deer has yet to be introduced into a truly wild area, it remains unknown whether it still retains enough of its natural instincts to survive on its own. In experiments where the Deer are exposed to the scents of Tiger skins and recorded big cat roaring, they show appropriate alarm behavior and wariness, demonstrating that they still recognize them as predators. But it remains to be seen whether enough of their untamed instincts are still intact to successfully deal with the danger in the wild. If the Père David's Deer proves to be unable to adapt to its natural lifestyle, it may survive only as a semi-domesticated animal, an inhabitant of Zoos and protected preserves, unable to live free on its own.

KANSAS CITY ZOO
Kansas City MO

In its early years, Kansas City was a wild frontier town. First settled by French fur traders, the little outpost was occupied by Mormons who were fleeing west, then turned into a shipping dock on the Mississippi River in 1833 and given the name Westport Landing. It quickly became important as a stop along the Sante Fe Trail, Oregon Trail, and California Trail. Seventeen years later, some land speculators moved in, bought up much of the property, and renamed it Kansas Town, after the nearby Kansas River.

Even before the Civil War began, Kansas was the scene of vicious fighting between pro-slavery and anti-slavery "militias", and the Confederates made unsuccessful attempts to invade the state. After the war, Kansas Town and Westport both became important transportation centers, as cargo and passengers arrived by boat and then were carried across the West by railroad. In 1889 the two towns merged to form Kansas City.

In the 1890s and 1900s, Kansas City became the domain of Tom Pendergast, the wealthy baron who controlled the city's political machine. Corrupt to the core, "Boss Tom" allowed the local vice to run rampant, and Kansas City became widely known as a den of gambling, prostitution, and (during

Prohibition) bootleg booze. One newspaper in Omaha declared, "If you want to see some sin, forget about Paris and go to Kansas City." It earned the town the nickname "Paris of the Plains". It was not meant as a compliment.

By the early 1900s the city was looking to polish its image a bit, and decided that a Zoo would help. "Kansas City cannot be a metropolitan," declared the Chamber of Commerce, "without a zoological garden." Boss Tom agreed to set aside 60 acres of land inside Swope Park, a Zoological Society was formed in 1907, and in December 1909 the Kansas City Zoological Gardens opened. It consisted of a duck pond and one building which housed four Lions, three monkeys, a Wolf, a Fox, a Coyote, a Badger, a Lynx, and assorted birds including a Bald Eagle. Very quickly, it was decided to expand the Zoo with an open-air exhibit, and the Bear Grotto was opened in 1912. There was subsequently some excitement when a Grizzly Bear named Nemo, who had been captured in Yellowstone National Park and given to the Zoo, managed to scale the walls of the Bear Grotto and escape. He was found a few weeks later sleeping in the city cemetery.

Through the Roaring Twenties and Prohibition, Kansas City thrived. Its many nightclubs and speakeasies made it a center for jazz music that rivaled New Orleans. In 1935, Boss Tom Pendergast was arrested for tax evasion and went to jail. The city was less unfortunate—the demand for its services as a transport center for beef cattle, wheat and corn, guaranteed that Kansas City made it through the Great Depression in better shape than most other cities. The WPA did build a new Monkey Island in the Zoo, though.

After World War II, the Zoo grew steadily, as did the city. In 1948 a new children's Zoo (named "Touchtown") was built, which had farm animals and a Noah's Ark. Later, a birthday pavilion and a puppet theater were added. These were followed over the next few decades by a Sea Lion pool, an Elephant House and Great Ape House, and islands for the Gibbons.

In 1991, Kansas City's residents approved a referendum to issue $50 million in bonds to raise money for the Zoo, and a massive expansion followed. The size of the facility was increased to 202 acres, and new "Africa" and "Australia" exhibit areas were constructed, followed by the "International Festival". Kansas City also became the first Zoo to have its own IMAX theater (though this was closed a few years later). By 1998 there were almost 750,000 visitors a year.

In 2002, the management of the Zoo was turned over to the Friends Of The Zoo organization, and another $30 million bond issue led to more expansions under a new Zoo Director. Orangutan Primadome opened, followed by Discovery Barn, the Tropics House, Tiger Trail, a new Sea Lion Pavilion, and Penguin Plaza, as well as a new remodeled front entrance. In 2011 the City passed a special sales tax increase to provide funding for the Zoo. By 2020, Kansas City was making most of the "Top Ten Zoo" lists.

The Zoo is also involved with several Species Survival Plans, and one of these is for an animal that most people pay little attention to: the Wyoming Toad.

The amphibians were some of the earliest animals on Earth to emerge from the water and live on land, when fishlike vertebrates like *Tiktaalik* crawled out onto the mud at least 350 million years ago. They evolved to become the modern frogs, toads and salamanders.

Typically, toads are differentiated from frogs by their lifestyles: while frogs tend to stay in water, toads are more terrestrial and often wander far from water. Toads also usually have rough dry warty skin, and are protected from predators by two large poison-filled paratoid glands on the back of their neck.

But even today, the amphibian adaptation for life on land is not complete. No matter where they live, amphibians must return to water in order to lay eggs and reproduce. Also, amphibian skins are not waterproof. This allows them to easily absorb body moisture without needing to drink, but it also leaves them very vulnerable to environmental contaminants.

Worldwide, frogs and toads are in serious trouble, and nobody is quite sure why. In the 1970s, however, biologists around the world began to notice significant declines in the populations of frogs and toads. Some species, such as the Panamanian Golden Toad, dwindled and then disappeared entirely. By the 1990s, virtually every species of frog on the planet had declined measurably, and many were now endangered. Frantic field studies were launched to try to solve the mystery and a number of causes have been proposed, ranging from pollution by industrial toxins, to hormonal changes caused by chemicals in the water, to the spread of new parasites, fungus or bacteria into areas where they did not exist before. None of these proposals explains all of the declines, though, and it may be that there are a number of different factors at work simultaneously which are affecting each species differently. (Though one common thread that seems to run through all of the proposed mechanisms is warming average temperatures produced by climate change.)

One of the amphibian species that has had a population crash is the Wyoming Toad, *Anaxyrus baxteri*. It is not the only declining amphibian in the US—there are dozens of others—but this time the problem is even more drastic since this rare Toad is found in only one location in the world: the Laramie Basin in Wyoming.

During the last Ice Age, most of the northern United States was covered with huge sheets of ice over a mile thick. Nothing could live there. But when the glaciers melted and retreated some 13,000 years ago, they left isolated patches of gouges that filled in with water and became ponds and lakes. For amphibians, which need water to lay eggs, these became refuges where they could live and thrive, surrounded by the hot dry Great Plains that were hostile to frogs and toads.

One of these glacial waters is Mortenson Lake, located near Laramie WY in Albany County. Here, isolated in the Laramie Basin from other populations, a group of toads survived and became a separate gene pool. Using the wetlands and floodplains around Mortenson Lake as a breeding ground, the Wyoming Toads became locally common, with a healthy population that hibernated through the brutal Plains winters, then emerged in spring to hop around in the surrounding grassland eating bugs and laying their gelatinous mass of eggs in ponds, pools and puddles.

Things changed in the 1970s, when the population suddenly began to decline, then plummeted. By 1980 researchers were only able to find 25 individuals, total. The Wyoming Toad was on the verge of disappearing entirely.

Wildlife officials and biologists rushed to figure out what was going on. Some studies pointed to insecticides that were being used for mosquito control, others pointed to changes in water level caused by agricultural irrigation, and still others pointed to the drying effects of climate change. In 1980 a type of fungus known as "chytrid" was found infecting the toads and these were known to be lethal, and in 1990 a bacteria that was known to be fatal to amphibians was also found in the lake, but it is not clear whether either of these were the original cause of the decline, or whether they were just opportunistically attacking an already-weakened population.

By January 1984 the Wyoming Toad was placed on the Endangered Species List and the Wyoming Toad Recovery Group was formed to draw up a plan to save it. Wildlife officials worked with local agencies to reduce insecticide use in areas inhabited by the Toads, and potential habitat area was protected by the Mortenson Lake National Wildlife Refuge. The Saratoga National Fish Hatchery was tasked with breeding the Toads and raising tadpoles for release into the wild, and they developed hormonal methods of increasing the output and survivability of eggs. Each female Toad produces thousands of eggs, but most of them don't survive to maturity. In 1993, twelve adult Toads were captured and added to the captive-breeding program. These were the last wild Wyoming Toads that anyone ever saw, and the species was listed later as "Extinct in the Wild".

A number of Zoos also participated in the captive-breeding program, including Denver and Kansas City. Tens of thousands of human-reared tadpoles were released into the Mortenson Lake National Wildlife Refuge, the George Lake National Wildlife Refuge, and an undisclosed privately-owned lake in the area.

At first, the program seemed to be successful. In 1998, the mating calls of Wyoming Toads could be heard in the release area and several egg masses were found over the next few years, indicating that the captive-bred Toads were successfully breeding in the wild.

But then things took a downturn. It was found that the entire habitat was infected by chytrid fungus and the Toads could not avoid it. Some 40% of all the wild adults were infected, and the fungus also spread to much of the captive population. Researchers also found that none of the wild individuals were living more than three years. Despite the nearly 100,000 tadpoles that had been released, the population of wild adults had not grown, and surveys were only able to find a couple dozen. It was apparent that even these numbers were only being maintained by the constant reintroduction of thousands of new captive-bred tadpoles each year.

The future of the Wyoming Toad still remains uncertain.

LEHIGH VALLEY ZOO
Allentown PA

At just 29 acres displaying 250 animals of 70 species, the Lehigh Valley Zoo is one of the smallest zoological gardens in the United States. But that did not prevent its founder from playing a unique conservation role.

When Columbus landed in the New World in 1492, the American Bison (*Bison bison*), also known as the Buffalo, was probably the most numerous mammal in North America. Vast herds roamed the Great Plains from Canada down to Texas, and various subspecies inhabited forests as far east as Pennsylvania. Bison even penetrated the swamplands of Florida. By some estimates there may have been over 60 million individuals.

Paleo-Indians in North America were hunting various species of Bison for well over 10,000 years. But the modern species *Bison bison* was of particular importance to the Natives of the Great Plains. The animals provided tribes like the Lakota, Pawnee and Crow with virtually everything they needed: smoked and dried bison meat provided them with food through the winter, buffalo skin robes offered warmth, hide tents served as the Plains tipi shelter, and bison bones and horns yielded tools and utensils. For thousands of years, Native hunters and their dogs tracked the Bison herds, and when the Spaniards introduced horses to the continent, the tribes were quick to size the advantage. Entire villages were nomadic, migrating to follow the great herds of Buffalo that dotted the plains.

Then the Europeans came. Some wanted land for farms. Some wanted wagon trails and railroads to go further west. Some wanted gold. Some wanted an anonymous new life in some small frontier town. But one thing they *all* wanted was for the "Indians" to be gone.

There followed a virtual war of extermination. One by one, the Plains tribes were slaughtered. And the Bison fell victim too. The eastern woods Bison had long ago fallen before the plow and axe: now the western plains Buffalo would be targeted too. The American settlers recognized that without the resources provided by the Bison herds there could be no free-living Native people, and the vast numbers of shaggy beasts were systematically destroyed. Some were shot for their hide, some were shot for their tongue, most were just shot and left to rot. Photos from the time show colossal piles of skulls, tens of thousands of them, waiting to be ground into powder and sold as fertilizer. By 1890, the Plains tribes had all surrendered. And of the 60 million or so Bison that had roamed North America, less than 600 could still be found. It was ecological warfare on an immense scale.

When Teddy Roosevelt traveled west in the 1880s on a hunting trip, he was shocked at what he saw. Or, rather, what he did *not* see. Roosevelt had not yet ridden up San Juan Hill or become the trust-busting President of the United States, but he was already famous as an adventurer and big-game hunter who had shot animals in faraway Africa and South America— many for museum displays. But when he got to the Dakotas, he was shaken to see that there was not a living Bison anywhere in sight. All of the vast herds that he had read so much about were gone.

Roosevelt became a one-person conservation campaign. With his friend zoo director William Temple Hornaday, he formed the American Bison Society for the express goal of protecting the remaining Bison herds, expanding them, and reintroducing them back into the wild. But his vision went much further. When he became President, Roosevelt championed the idea of "National Parks" and "National Wildlife Refuges", and set aside natural areas for preservation. His ideas helped inspire others, and in quick succession a number of environmental groups appeared including the National Audubon Society and the Sierra Club. With the help of Hornaday and the Bison Society, new herds were established in Yellowstone National Park, the National Bison Range in Montana, and the Wichita Mountains Wildlife Refuge.

In the Lehigh River Valley in eastern Pennsylvania, Harry Clay Trexler had similar ideas. Trexler had become wealthy on timber sales and cement mills and, like Teddy Roosevelt, he was a gentleman-sportsman who had gone on hunting expeditions to the Plains, and was profoundly affected by the imminent extinction of some of America's most prominent animals. Trexler purchased 24 farmsteads in the tiny hamlet of Schnecksville, just outside Allentown, totaling some 2500 acres. Surrounding these areas with fence, he dug up the ground and replanted it with grass and began buying up as many native Pennsylvania game animals as he could find— White-Tail Deer, Elk, and (when he learned that they were in fact once found in Pennsylvania) Bison. By 1923 his "Deer Reservation" had expanded to 7,000 acres.

When Trexler unexpectedly died in 1933, his will stipulated that his wild animal refuge, now renamed "Trexler Game Preserve", be donated to Lehigh County "for use as a public park" and that it be a permanent home for his herd of Bison, now numbering 98.

Hornaday, meanwhile, was also having success with his Bison. Now Director of the Bronx Zoo, he sent part of his Buffalo collection to Montana to establish a new wild herd and continued to speak out on behalf of wildlife conservation.

Seemingly, the fight to save the Bison was a smashing success. From a population as low as 540 individuals in 1890, there are now over half a million Buffalo in the hands of private ranchers and some 30,000 in national or state parks.

But things are not as good as it might appear.

Most of the people who set aside land for Bison, like Trexler, had good intentions, but they were inexperienced in wildlife management. Often, ranches would allow their Bison and domestic Cattle to intermingle. Although the two species are not all that closely related, they are capable of interbreeding, and this meant that much of the original founding Bison populations were mating with the ranch Cattle that shared their enclosures. In many cases this was done on purpose by ranchers as a misguided conservation measure: it was hoped that Bison/Cattle matings might produce "hybrid vigor" which would fight the effects of the Buffalo's diminished gene pool and help save the species.

As a result of all this interbreeding, however, only some 15,000 or so of today's Bison—the descendants of herds that were kept strictly isolated—still have pure *Bison bison* genes. All the rest are hybridized to some extent and carry some proportion of domestic Cattle genes. For most of the Bison that are alive today, this doesn't matter much. The vast majority of today's Buffalo are more or less domesticated and live on ranches, where they are raised for hides or for meats. In many cases the two species are now intentionally hybridized to produce "beefalo", a specialty which tastes similar to beef but is lower in fat. But if the goal is to produce Bison herds for reintroduction to the prairies, it is important that the gene lines be kept purely wild. On the other hand, however, a pure strain of Bision, with its small founding population, would suffer from the debilitating effects of inbreeding within a group that had a serious lack of genetic diversity. It puts the whole issue in a dilemma.

The breeding success enjoyed by the various Federal and state programs, meanwhile, meant that the little herd of 100 or so in the Trexler Preserve was losing its importance, and it began to dwindle. At one point the herd became infected with a lung disease: most of the Bison died and had to be replaced. The Preserve itself was never really a priority with the local government, and was open to visitors only one day a week. In 1975, Lehigh County opened a small petting zoo inside the Preserve with animals from Asia, Australia, and Africa, grandly named the Lehigh Valley Zoo, to try to attract more paying guests to defray expenses, but construction costs soared to $2 million and the hoped-for visitorship of 650,000 a year barely exceeded 100,000.

By 2004, with both the Preserve and the County in appalling financial shape, a proposal was introduced to close down the petting zoo entirely. The Trexler Trust, meanwhile, sued the county government for violating the terms of the Trexler bequest by not making the Preserve available to the public (which the County simply didn't have the money to do). A year later a settlement was agreed to: the Lehigh Valley Zoo would be turned over to a nonprofit Zoological Society, and the rest of the 1,000-acre Preserve would be fully opened to the public as a park with hiking trails and picnic facilities. The County would contribute $1.9 million for this and the Trexler Trust would donate a further $850,000.

Under the Zoological Society, a fundraising effort was launched to expand the revamped Lehigh Valley Zoo, and new enclosures were built for a variety of animals. By 2020 the Zoo was AZA certified and was a participant in three Species Survival Plans, for the African Jackass Penguin, the Scimitar-Horned Oryx, and the Mongoose Lemur. And there is still a herd of around a dozen American Bison on display, descendents of Trexler's original group.

MONTEREY AQUARIUM
San Francisco CA

For many years, San Francisco's economy was centered on Cannery Row. The rich waters off the California coast provided huge catches of fish, especially sardines, and by 1902 a whole series of commercial canneries had opened along the waterfront to pack and sell them. During the two World Wars, the canneries were working overtime to fill the demand from both the military, who issued canned fish as part of soldiers' rations, and the stateside civilian work force, who used it as cheap wartime food.

But by the 1950s the glory days of the canneries were finished. Overfishing had depleted the fish supply, and the sardine schools moved elsewhere. One by one, the cannery companies closed down, and the waterfront area became a rundown derelict. In the 1970s, a number of tourist shops, hotels, and restaurants moved into Cannery Row, but there were still several abandoned fish-packing buildings remaining. One of these was the Hovden Cannery, which had been founded during the First World War and had gone out of business in 1973.

Around this time, four marine biologists from Stanford University and San Jose State University began talking about the possibility of establishing a public Aquarium on the

Cannery Row waterfront. Similar proposals had been made before but had always failed for lack of funding. But this time things were different. By the late 1970s, the computer industry was big business, Silicon Valley was producing millionaires almost as fast as computers, and California was at the center of it all. As it turned out, one of the four biologists had a particularly influential and wealthy parent—David Packard, one of the founders of the Hewlett-Packard computer company. In April 1978, Packard formed the Monterey Bay Aquarium Foundation, bought the old Hovden Cannery, and set aside $7 million to build an Aquarium. (After a research trip to several large Aquariums in Japan, that budget grew to $55 million.)

Rather than tearing down the old cannery, plans called for as much of the historic building to be preserved as possible. The old warehouse would be remodeled into offices and workspaces for the Aquarium's administrators, while the pump house that used to bring sardines up from water level into the cannery was now occupied by the giant pipes, valves and suction pumps that would draw in 2,000 gallons per minute of new sea water, to be treated and circulated through all of the exhibits and holding tanks before being discharged back into the Bay. The entire system had to be designed from scratch, including a method for cleaning out the pipes and removing any blockages. All of the pumps and filters were computer-controlled. During the day the incoming seawater would be filtered for clarity, guaranteeing that guests would have a good view inside the display tanks; at night the system would run unfiltered water through the tanks to duplicate a natural habitat.

Much of the Aquarium was constructed out over the water, and a number of outdoor walkways and decks allowed visitors to look out over the open Bay, where an artificial tide pool was built and where wild Sea Lions, Sea Otters and a variety of ocean birds could often be seen.

The Monterey Bay Aquarium opened in October 1984, with 83 tanks exhibited in 12 galleries, the largest in the US at the time. Unlike the other existing public Aquariums, which displayed tropical reef fish and sharks from all over the world, Monterey was unique in focusing almost exclusively on the local native species that live within the natural ecosystems of San Francisco Bay. The facility was also specifically designed with the intent to carry out scientific research in the Bay, and this led to the establishment of the Monterey Bay National Marine Sanctuary in 1992.

The Aquarium's centerpiece is the 320,000-gallon Kelp Forest display, which stands 28 feet tall. Kelp is a kind of marine algae that forms dense underwater stands and provides food and shelter for a wide variety of fish and other ocean life. Because Kelp requires moving water to survive, the display was only made possible by Monterey's unique system of constantly-circulating seawater, supplemented by natural sunlight and a "surge machine" which duplicates wave action. The exhibit contains a variety of native fish that can be found in the kelp forest, including Rock Fish, Garibaldi Fish, and Leopard Sharks.

The other large exhibit is the 1.2 million gallon Open Sea gallery, which houses species that are found further away from the California coast in the deep ocean. There are Bluefin Tuna, Hammerhead Sharks, Mahi-Mahi, Pacific Mackerel, Ocean Sunfish, Sea Turtles, and schools of sardines. In July 2011, all of the 10,000 or so individual animals in this exhibit were caught and temporarily relocated so the entire tank could be drained for a $20 million renovation.

Smaller tanks and pools house a variety of other marine species. The Monterey Bay Habitats exhibit contains a series of tanks illustrating the variety of different ecosystems found in the Bay, from shallow-water beaches all the way out to the deep ocean. Another exhibit holds a colony of California Sea Lions, and some of the rescued Sea Otters are also on view in their own 55,000-gallon tank. Other displays contain Sea Jellies, Penguins, Sponges, Anemones, Sea Stars, Lobsters, and Pelicans.

In addition to the permanent displays, the Aquarium hosts temporary exhibits from year to year. These sometimes focus on particular groups of animals (such as Octopus, Jellyfish, and Sea Horses) or on a particular geographic area (like the Baja California and the Sea of Cortez).

In 1986, the Monterey Aquarium was used as a location for filming the Hollywood blockbuster "Star Trek IV: The Voyage

Home", standing in as abode for the Humpback Whales which were central to the movie's plot. Monterey does not actually keep any whales, Orcas or Dolphins and does not have any tank suitable for that. Instead, the movie's whale scenes were filmed on the Aquarium's outdoors observation decks, and a miniature "whale tank", complete with lifelike moveable molded-rubber models of Humpback Whales, was inserted into the finished shots using greenscreen FX technology.

From the beginning, the Aquarium had planned to do scientific research and wildlife rescue for local species. In cooperation with Stanford University's Hopkins Marine Station, the Aquarium carries out research on Pacific Bluefin Tuna populations in the wild. Monterey's colony of African Penguins are captive-bred as part of the Species Survival Plan for the endangered birds. The Aquarium also partners with the Point Blue Conservation Science program to collect eggs from the local endangered Snowy Plover, artificially incubate them, and then release the chicks to the wild when they are big enough.

By the time the Aquarium finished construction in 1984, it had already established the Sea Otter Research and Conservation Program, which takes in injured or orphaned Sea Otters, rehabilitates them, and returns the animals back to the wild.

The Sea Otter (*Enhydra lutris*) is a member of the Mustelid family which includes Skunks, Weasels and Minks. They are related to the freshwater River Otters, but unlike their freshwater cousins the Sea Otters are marine animals. The Sea Otters are also much larger, weighing in at up to 100 pounds. There are three subspecies ranging from Japan around the northern Pacific to Russia, Alaska, and down the North American west coast. The variety found in California is the Southern Sea Otter, *Enhydra lutris nereis*.

Unlike their terrestrial cousins, Sea Otters are entirely aquatic and can live their entire lives in the coastal ocean, never touching land. To help with swimming and diving, the Otters have webbed feet and exceptionally dense bones which act like dive weights. They make their living by diving to the ocean floor for shellfish, which they bring to the surface and eat while floating on their back—using a rock as a tool to pound the shells and break them open. (This makes the Otters one of the few nonhuman animals to use tools.) Once they find a particularly good rock, they are able to carry it around with them by tucking it into a loose fold of skin under their armpits.

Unlike whales or seals, however, Sea Otters have no insulating layer of blubber or body fat. So to protect themselves from the icy cold water, they have evolved an incredibly dense and thick coat of waterproof fur which traps air and keeps the water away from the skin.

Unfortunately, the same properties that make the Otter's pelt so suitable for conditions in the Pacific Ocean also make it desirable for human-produced fur hats and coats, and from the early 18th century the animals were hunted relentlessly. Once estimated at around 250,000 or more, the global population of Sea Otters was reduced to barely more than 1,000 by 1900. A ban on hunting has allowed the numbers to rebound somewhat, and the global population now is estimated at around 125,000. This distribution is patchy however, and only scattered colonies can be found in Mexico, California, Oregon, Washington, British Columbia, and Alaska. The Otters still remain rare or absent on some parts of their former range.

In 1973 the Sea Otter was protected by the Endangered Species Act and conservation efforts were begun. Over the years Sea Otters have been reintroduced to some portions of their former habitat, with varying degrees of success.

In California, hunters from Russia and Alaska had wiped out nearly all of the Sea Otters by 1905, and the animals were assumed to be extinct in the state. Then in 1938 a small isolated colony of around 50 individuals was found near Big Sur. These were given immediate protection. Sea Otters are ecologically important along the California coast because they eat a lot of Sea Urchins, which would otherwise graze on the Giant Kelp forests and reduce this important habitat.

In the 1980s, Federal wildlife officials relocated 140 Sea Otters to San Nicolas Island off the southern California coast, hoping to establish a population that would remain safe from any oil spills. (Sea Otters are very vulnerable to spills because they constantly lick their fur to keep it clean and waterproof, which would cause them to swallow fatal amounts of oil.)

Instead, most of the Otters dispersed, with some swimming back to the mainland coast and the rest going to other islands. Overall the California population grew, reaching a bit less than 3,000 and spreading as far south as San Diego. But the growth rate is still slow, there have been several reverses, and it is apparent that a real recovery is still off in the future. When Abalone fishermen complained that the Otters were eating their stocks, the Fish and Wildlife Service set up "no otter zones" in which any wild Sea Otters would be trapped and relocated, but this effort never worked well, and the Abalone fishery died out anyway due to declining catches caused by climate change and by overharvesting.

At the Monterey Aquarium, the Sea Otter rescue program has been successful. From 1984 to 2020, the facility has rehabilitated and released over 800 injured or orphaned Otters. Animals that are unable to make a complete recovery are given a permanent home at the Aquarium or other institutions, where they are placed on exhibit as "animal ambassadors" to help educate people about Sea Otter conservation. (The Monterey Otter exhibit is live-streamed on the Internet 24 hours a day.)

One of the issues faced by the Aquarium was that many of the rescued orphan pups were too young to have been taught all they need to know by their mother, and because of this inexperience they would not survive in the wild. In response, the staff began a program of using adult females from the captive breeding program (mostly unreleasable individuals) to serve as "foster parents" for the immature orphans. This innovation has resulted in around 40 young Otters being released into Monterey Bay that could not otherwise have been returned to the wild.

The Monterey Aquarium receives about 2.5 million visitors a year and is one of the most popular attractions in California.

SEA WORLD
Orlando FL, San Diego CA, San Antonio TX

In 1963, four recently-graduated students from UCLA decided to go into business together. Their idea was for an underwater luxury restaurant built on the California coast, which would also exhibit fish and marine life in large aquarium tanks. They would call it "Sea World".

When they started putting pencil to paper and pricing out actual designs, however, the project turned out to be too ambitious and too expensive. Switching gears, they decided upon a marine park instead, similar to Marineland in Florida, with Dolphins and ocean fish. They obtained 22 acres of land in San Diego and began construction of displays, pools, and holding tanks. When Sea World opened in March 1964, it had Dolphins, reef fish, and California Sea Lions.

It was wildly successful, with over 400,000 visitors in its first year. In 1968, the company went public, and the stock issues raised a ton of money that could be reinvested in growth. The four partners quickly made plans to expand into a new location which was closer to the population centers in the northeast. As it turned out, their choice of location—Aurora OH, near Cleveland—was a poor decision. The new Sea World Ohio was larger and had more animals (Orcas, or Killer Whales, were just beginning to be kept successfully in captivity), but the area's brutal northern winters meant that the park could only open for visitors in the summer months.

The Ohio park debuted in 1970. A year later, Walt Disney World appeared in Orlando FL and changed the face of tourist resorts. More importantly for Sea World, Disney killed off many of the old traditional Florida attractions, including Marineland. The field was now wide open, and Sea World jumped in. Plans were quickly made for a new park in Florida which would take advantage of the huge stream of visitors drawn in by Disney. Sea World Orlando opened in 1973.

By now, most of Sea World's attractions (and advertising) centered around its collection of Orcas. Orcas, also known as Killer Whales, are not actually whales but are the largest members of the dolphin family. Highly intelligent and social animals, they live together in packs called "pods" where they hunt together for prey ranging from large fish to small whales. Sea World's staff of marine biologists, behaviorists and veterinarians soon learned how to keep and care for Orcas in captivity. The captive breeding program was so successful that it was no longer necessary to capture Orcas from the wild. These captive-bred Orcas were trained to do shows that were immensely popular with visitors, with all the Orcas performing under the stage name "Shamu".

Sea World also became one of the country's largest marine rescue and rehabilitation centers. Teams of rescuers were organized to respond to whale strandings, orphaned or sick Dolphins, and injured Sea Turtles or other marine animals, which were brought in, treated and, if possible, released back to the wild.

At Sea World Orlando, much of the rescue effort focuses on the native species of endangered Sea Turtles. Five species of turtle inhabit Florida's coastal marine waters: the Leatherback, the Loggerhead, the Green Turtle, the Kemp's Ridley, and the Hawksbill. Three of these, the Leatherback, Green, and Loggerhead, regularly breed on Florida's beaches: the rest either do not nest there or only do so sporadically.

Leatherback Sea Turtle (*Dermochelys coriacea*)
The Leatherback is so different from all the other living Sea Turtles that it is placed by itself in a separate family. Even in

appearance it is unique: instead of the familiar turtle shell, the Leatherback, as the name implies, has a sleek leathery body with seven distinct ridges that run along its back. This is just one of the biological traits which demonstrate that these turtles are highly adapted for an aquatic life. The flippers, for instance, have lost the remnants of terrestrial toenails that other sea turtles still have. Although all Sea Turtles can excrete excess salt from glands in their eyes, Leatherbacks have become adapted to a level of salt in their body tissues almost twice as high as other Sea Turtles.

The Leatherback also has the ability to both produce body heat through muscular contractions and to use its large body mass to retain it, which allows them to maintain enough metabolic heat energy to remain active even in cold waters. The species therefore has a very wide range, through the Atlantic, Pacific and Indian oceans, as far north as Alaska, while the other Sea Turtles are mostly limited to warm waters.

At a length of six feet (sometimes reaching ten feet) and a weight of up to a full ton, the Leatherback is the largest of the Sea Turtles, and one of the heaviest of reptiles. Despite this, it begins life in an egg that is not much bigger than an ordinary ping-pong ball. Although they are well-suited for a life in the ocean, the females must still come shore to nest. Florida is just one of the places where this species breeds during the summer, and it is estimated that there are around 50 nesting females here each year. Hauling her huge bulk onto the beach at night, the female will dig a deep cavity in the sand and deposit her eggs before covering them up and lumbering back to the water. When the young turtles emerge about two months later, they must dig themselves out of the sand and cross the gauntlet of open beach before reaching the relative safety of the sea.

Leatherbacks feed almost exclusively on jellyfish, which they able to seize and swallow with the help of spiny growths on the inside of the throat. Since these animals are low in food value, the huge Leatherbacks must eat a lot of jellies each day.

Loggerhead Sea Turtle (*Caretta caretta*)

The Loggerhead is the most common Sea Turtle found in Florida waters, especially during the nesting season. It is estimated that about 80% of all the Loggerheads in the world make their nest at a Florida beach on either the Atlantic or Gulf Coast—some 70,000 nests each year. (There is another large nesting area in Oman on the shores of the Mediterranean.) A fullgrown adult can reach about three feet in length and weigh a bit less than 300 pounds, which makes it one of the larger species—though nowhere near as big as the Leatherback.

The name comes from the relatively large head, which houses powerful muscles needed to crush the shellfish which the Loggerhead feeds on.

Green Turtle (*Chelonia mydas*)

The name Green Turtle comes not from the shell, but from the green body fat under the inside of the shell which was used to make turtle soup. The eggs were also considered a delicacy, and shortly after the Europeans arrived in Florida they began exporting processed turtles back to England and Spain. It decimated the population.

Today, like nearly all the Sea Turtles, the Green Turtle is severely endangered. While Florida's Sea Turtles are no longer hunted, they still face serious threats from loss of breeding sites and from human activity on the remaining beaches. In the open oceans, Sea Turtles are often trapped inside fishing and trawling nets where they drown, and to prevent this commercial fishing nets are now required to have Turtle Exclusion Devices (TEDs) which allow them to escape.

Green Sea Turtles are often found inhabiting offshore reefs in relatively shallow water, where they feed on sea grass, algae, seaweed, and other aquatic plants. It is estimated that at least 1000-2000 Green Sea Turtle nests are laid on Florida beaches each year, making this one of their most important breeding grounds. (Though the majority nest in the Caribbean and Central America, especially Costa Rica.)

Hawksbill (*Eretmochelys imbricata*)

At a length of around 2.5 feet and a weight of 150 pounds, this is one of the smallest of the Sea Turtles. The Hawksbill prefers very warm tropical waters of the Atlantic, Pacific and Indian Oceans, and is usually found only sporadically in Florida, mostly in the Keys. The turtles nest mostly in Australia, Oman and the Caribbean.

Like the Green Sea Turtle, the Hawksbill was heavily exploited commercially—not for food, but for the highly polished and multi-colored shell, the source of the "tortoiseshell" that was once widely used to make combs, jewelry, and ornaments.

Today the trade in "tortoiseshell" has been banned by international law and the material has been replaced by plastics, but the Hawksbill remains endangered. The turtle's principle food is sponges, which it pulls from rocks and reefs.

Kemp's Ridley Sea Turtle (*Lepidochelys kempi*)

The smallest of the living Sea Turtles, Kemp's Ridley Sea Turtle is also the rarest and the most endangered. It is estimated that less than 1000 breeding females still exist, worldwide.

Although it can sometimes be seen in the Keys, where it hunts for crabs, the Kemp's turtle does not breed in Florida. Indeed until 1947 it was not known at all where they nested, until they were found on a single remote beach in Mexico—and this remains their only natural nesting site.

In the 1980s, an effort was made to help protect this species by collecting several thousand eggs from Mexico, incubating them and then artificially planting them on a beach in Texas. Since breeding turtles always return to the beach where they themselves hatched, it was hoped that these new Kemp's Ridley hatchlings would, when they grow up, return to Texas to nest, thereby establishing another breeding spot. But at that time not much was known about Sea Turtle biology, including the fact that their sex is determined by the temperature they are incubated at—so nearly all of the hatchlings turned out to be males. The few of the youngsters who were female apparently all died in the wild. None returned to nest.

Since then, as knowledge has increased and methods have gotten better, there has been some success: as of 2007, some 150 Kemp's Ridley Sea Turtles were nesting on Texas beaches. The effort continues.

In 1976, the Harcourt Brace Jovanovich company, a book publisher which specialized in educational textbooks, was looking to expand, and they bought Sea World. Plans were immediately made for a new park, which opened in San Antonio TX in 1988, but this, like the Ohio park, turned out to be a poor choice of location. Unlike the San Diego and Orlando parks, which thrived, the San Antonio park never got the number of visitors that HBJ had expected, and it switched to a seasonal schedule, closing for most of the winter. Harcourt Brace Jovanovich was soon looking to get out, and in 1989 it reached an agreement with the Annheuser-Busch Company, the huge beer brewery that already owned the Busch Gardens parks. Busch bought all four of the Sea World locations as well as two other smaller attractions in Florida owned by HBJ—Cypress Gardens in Winter Haven and Boardwalk and Baseball in Haines City.

Annheuser-Busch upgraded the Sea World parks, adding roller coasters and more shows in an effort to attract more young people and families. The Ohio location, which had always been crippled by the weather, was sold to the Six Flags Company and combined with another amusement park, reappearing as a conventional water park. There were plans for A-B to make up for this with a new Sea World in the tourist city of Abu Dhabi in the United Arab Emirates, but that idea was shelved during the 2008 Great Recession and the 2020 Covid pandemic. In the end, Annheuser-Busch was itself purchased by In-Bev, which then sold Sea World along with the Busch Gardens parks to a series of owners.

However, during this time the Sea World parks also began to face increasing criticism, as animal rights activists targeted the practice of keeping intelligent social animals like Orcas in captivity. The film "Blackfish" was produced which, while inaccurate in some parts, had a large public impact that increased in 2010 when one of the keepers at Sea World was killed by an Orca. In 2016, Sea World announced that they would no longer breed Orcas and would no longer do public "Shamu" shows, and would eventually phase the Orcas out of the parks.

SHEDD AQUARIUM
Chicago IL

In 1924, the Chicago Zoological Society was already three years old and was still laying plans and seeking support for a Zoo in Chicago. But John Shedd, who was the President of the giant Marshall Field department store company, decided that this would not be enough—a city such as Chicago should, he thought, also have an Aquarium. So with initial funding of $2 million, Shedd formed the Shedd Aquarium Society. The nonprofit's charter set its goal as "to construct, maintain and operate an aquarium or museum of aquatic life exclusively for educational and scientific purposes."

A short while later, the City donated a patch of land on the shore of Lake Michigan, right next to the Field Museum of Natural History, and planning could begin. Director Walter Chute made a world tour to visit some of the best Aquariums in Europe and Asia to examine and duplicate their state-of-the-art equipment and procedures, and incorporate the latest techniques into the design that was being put together by the Chicago firm of Graham, Anderson, Probst & White.

The Shedd Aquarium was to be a domed building in Greek style, of marble and terra cotta, to match the architecture of the Field Museum (which had been designed by the same firm). The front façade would present Doric columns, while the glass dome would be topped by a sculpture of Neptune's trident. There would be a central octagonal rotunda with a 40-foot wide pool containing reef fish, surrounded by eight radiating bays which would exhibit both freshwater and saltwater species—a first for any inland Aquarium. Even the floor would be made from sheets of ancient limestone that was studded with marine fossils.

Unfortunately, Shedd died in October 1926 at age 76, while the Aquarium was still in the design stage. But the Society carried on, and construction began a year later. To provide the needed one million gallons of saltwater for the ocean tanks, a group of 20 tanker trains made the expedition from Chicago to Key West FL, returning full of natural sea water. It took eight round trips. In addition, a specially-made train car called "Nautilus" was equipped to carry live fish and other marine creatures back to Chicago for display. After a "Preview" in 1929, the Shedd Aquarium officially opened in May 1930 with 132 exhibits. It cost a total of $3 million, and was at the time the largest indoor Aquarium in the world.

In 1933 the World's Fair was held in Chicago, adjacent to the Aquarium, and Director Chute wanted some exotic animals to attract visitors. One of the exhibits he managed to obtain was a pair of Australian Lungfish. One of these, affectionately named "Granddad", then lived at Shedd for the next 84 years. When he died in 2017, Granddad was the oldest known Aquarium fish, with an age of at least 86 years.

In 1971, the 40-foot diameter reef pond in the central rotunda was modernized into a cylindrical walk-around tank of 95,000 gallons, containing reef fish, sea turtles, anemones and corals. In 2001, the Amazon Rising display was opened, which features fish, frogs, and turtles from South America including Piranha, Electric Eels, Mata-Mata and Caimans.

Since its opening the Shedd has undergone two major expansions. In 1991, the Oceanarium was added. With a motif reflecting the stylized art of the Pacific Northwest Native Americans, the Oceanarium was planned as a habitat for marine mammals, and contains pools and tanks for Belugas, Sea Lions, Sea Otters, Penguins, and Pacific White-Sided Dolphins. At the time it opened the Oceanarium was the largest indoors marine mammal facility in the world. In addition to shows and displays, the center served as a facility for rehabilitating marine mammals that were rescued by the Aquarium's "Animal Response Team", which can travel anywhere in the world to help stranded, injured, or orphaned sea animals.

In 2003 the Shedd expanded again with the opening of Wild Reef, built two floors beneath the original building. This exhibit featured a 400,000 gallon tank with several varieties of sharks, and additional tanks with corals and reef fish.

Meanwhile, the Aquarium was also focusing efforts on conservation. Shedd obtained its own ocean-going research ship, the *Coral Reef*, in 1971 and replaced that with the larger *Coral Reef II* in 1985. One of the Aquarium's research programs focuses on the Bahamian Rock Iguana in the Caribbean, and another centers on the various Sea Horse species in southeast Asia. The Shedd maintains a breeding colony of Beluga Whales in its Oceanarium area and studies them in the wild in Alaska's Bristol Bay.

Shedd also obtained four Pacific White-Sided Dolphins in May 1991, making it one of just three Aquariums in the US to keep this species. Since then a number of calves have been born as part of the captive-breeding program, the latest being "Harmony" who arrived in August 2020. The Aquarium often exchanges the Dolphins with the Miami SeaQuarium and Sea World San Antonio for breeding loans.

Of the 49 species of dolphin and porpoise, 11 can be found in the Pacific Ocean off the west coast of the United States. One of these is the Pacific White-Sided Dolphin (*Lagenorhynchus obliquidens*), known to most researchers as "Lags". These dolphins prefer somewhat cooler water and are found throughout the northern Pacific, from Japan up to the Aleutian Islands and down to California. There is a very similar White-Sided Dolphin species in the Atlantic which is slightly larger, though the Pacific Lag is genetically closer to the Dusky Dolphin from the southern Pacific, which probably evolved after the split between Atlantic and Pacific. Lags prefer to be in the open ocean and do not usually venture near shore. In the US, they appear to migrate seasonally, being more abundant in the north during summer and the south in the winter.

The Pacific Lags are one of the smaller of the dolphins, averaging 6-7 feet with males getting up to 8 feet. As the name suggests, they have a white stripe that runs along the side of their body from head to tail. The nose, or "rostrum", is relatively short. The sides and back are dark grey, and the belly is white. The dorsal fin is relatively tall and often has a curved end, which led to the name "Hook Porpoise", though they are not technically porpoises.

Like its more familiar cousin the Atlantic Bottlenose Dolphin, the Pacific White-Sided Dolphin is a highly-intelligent social creature. Individuals group together in pods that may contain as many as 100 members. They are curious and inquisitive creatures which are very active. Lags can swim at up to 25mph, and can often be seen riding the bow waves of ocean-going boats, which they can easily outrun. These dolphins are also prone to acrobatics and can often be seen jumping out of the water and doing a variety of spins, bellyflops, and somersaults.

Much of the diet consists of schooling fish, and the Lags will work together to capture them. Several members of the pod will surround the school and herd it together, allowing others to dart in and grab a mouthful. Like all dolphins they have short conelike teeth which are suited for seizing and holding slippery fish, and since they cannot chew their food they swallow it whole, headfirst so the fins don't get stuck. A typical adult eats about twenty pounds of fish a day.

By manipulating the air coming out of their blowholes, Pacific White-Sided Dolphins can produce a wide array of squeaks, squeals and clicks, which they use for communication. They are also able to produce bursts of high-frequency sound which acts as sonar, giving the dolphin an acoustical picture of what is around it. Like all mammals they are air-breathers, and periodically surface to breathe through their blowhole. On dives they can hold their breath for as long as six minutes.

Because they are dwellers of the open ocean, Pacific White-Sided Dolphins are not easy to study in the wild, and most of what we know about their biology comes from captive animals. They seem to have a lifespan of around 40 years and reach sexual maturity at about age 10. There is just one calf, who is carried for about a year before being born live, usually tail-first. The newborns are around three feet long and weigh around 30 pounds. They stay close to their mother to nurse, and can double their weight in just a few months.

In the wild, the only natural predator capable of catching a Pacific White-Sided Dolphin is the Orca or Killer Whale (which is actually a large dolphin rather than a true whale). The biggest threat to the Lags are humans. Japanese fishermen have long captured dolphins for food, and in modern times the mammals often became entangled in large drifting fishing nets and drowned. Such nets have now been banned. Although many dolphin species have declined and become threatened or endangered, the population of the White-Sided Dolphin appears to be large and stable, and they are considered a "Species of Least Concern". But like all dolphins they are protected by the Marine Mammal Act, and international trade is restricted by the CITES Treaty.

There are about 100 Pacific White-Sided Dolphins in captivity, most in Aquariums in Japan and China. Although the species is not endangered and there are no programs to reintroduce captive-bred animals, the human-raised individuals serve as educational "animal ambassadors", without the necessity of taking any individuals from the wild, to allow people to observe them and to learn about conservation of sea animals.

The Shedd Aquarium receives around 1.7 million visitors a year. In recognition of its celebrated architecture, the original domed building has been listed as a National Historic Landmark.

NEW ENGLAND AQUARIUM
Boston MA

Boston has always been focused on the sea. In colonial times, it was one of the continent's most important ports. The English colonies in North America had been founded as agricultural resources, and their primary products were tobacco, rice and cotton. But in the northeast, the soil was not well-suited for agriculture, and the economy there was turned towards the Atlantic Ocean. Maritime trade with Europe topped the list, followed by fishing.

After American independence, however, a new industry was beginning to take off. In an age before electricity, most homes were lit by oil lamps, and the best fuel for lamps came from whales. Fortunately for the colonists, the seas off the shores of Massachusetts had plenty of whales. To catch them, wooden towers were constructed along the shore, manned by lookouts. When a whale was spotted, a long rowboat (known as a "whaleboat") was launched from shore. Armed with iron harpoons and wooden floats, the men would paddle out and drive in as many harpoons as they could before the whale could dive away. When the huge animal became exhausted from dragging around the wooden floats, it would surface, and the whalers could kill it with lances, then tow the huge carcass back to shore to be processed.

A dead whale was enormously valuable. Ladies' fashion of the time required hoop skirts, corsets, and umbrella parasols, and these were made with strips of "whalebone", fringes of cartilaginous material found in the whale's mouth which were carefully trimmed out. The thick layer of blubber was cut off in large strips (a process called "flensing"), then sliced into smaller pieces which could be boiled in large iron kettles (known as "try pots") to render many barrels of whale oil. Finally, if the whalers were lucky enough to catch a Sperm Whale, the large cavity in the whale's head was filled with a thick waxy substance called "spermaceti", which could be used to make odorless and bright-burning candles that were far superior to ordinary tallow candles. Every typical household of the time had several different items, from shirt-collar stiffeners to horse buggy whips, that were made from whale products. A single whale could bring in a fortune and keep the entire town supplied for months.

By the 1820s, whale oil became even more important, as the early machinery of the nascent industrial age found a new use for it. Delicate machinery such as lathes, looms or steam engines needed constant lubrication, and whale oil was perfect for the purpose. As the demand for whale products grew, the industry expanded to meet it. And it was the Americans who were in the best position for this. With its rich timber resources and its communities of experienced merchant seamen, New England could build bigger ships and man them more easily than any other country, and soon American whaling vessels were dominating the trade. The enterprising Yankees found a way to take their "try pots" along with them to sea, perched atop large brick furnaces. By allowing the crew to extract whale oil right there aboard ship, the try pots freed them from their dependency on shore, allowing the larger American ships to stay at sea for three years or more at a time, traveling as far as the South Pacific in search of whales and returning with their entire hold stuffed full of barrels containing valuable whale oil. By the 1840s, there were over 700 vessels in the American whaling fleet.

By the time the Civil War ended in 1865, however, the Yankee whaling industry was already declining. A new and superior product—kerosene—was replacing whale oil as the lamp fuel of choice, while petroleum oil took its place as the best available machine lubricant. New technological innovations were also being made in Norway which gave their whaling fleet the edge in hunting down the already-dwindling supply of whales, including exploding-head harpoons and large iron-hulled "factory ships" that could process slaughtered whales more efficiently than the old wooden ships with their try-pots. But by far the most important factor was the drastic decline in whales themselves. Virtually every species had been hunted to the point of extinction. By 1895 the American whaling fleet had, like the whales themselves, virtually disappeared.

Given the importance of Boston's maritime history, then, it is perhaps not surprising that the city was the site for one of the first Aquariums in the US. Founded in 1859, the Boston Aquarial Gardens was a privately-owned for-profit venture that was set up by some local businessmen. It floundered for a year and a half before it was purchased by the city, relocated to Central Court and became the Boston Aquarial Gardens and Zoological Gardens. This zoo/aquarium closed down in 1863 because of financial pressures caused by the Civil War.

In 1912, the city decided to try another public Aquarium, and the South Boston Aquarium was opened. It continued until 1954, but it was hampered by a lack of funding, political disputes, and tight city control.

After the South Boston Aquarium ceased operations, a group of prominent citizens looked to an alternative model in which the city would provide funding but the Aquarium would be run independently by a nonprofit organization. In 1957, then, the New England Aquarium Corporation was formed with the express goal of creating a new public Aquarium in Boston. They obtained a tract of land on Central Wharf, in the neglected waterfront area, and began planning.

The New England Aquarium was designed around an immense circular central tank, surrounded by a multi-floor spiral staircase that wrapped around it. When the Aquarium officially opened in 1969, the Ocean Tank was not quite finished, but when it went on exhibit in 1970 it was the largest tank of its type in the world. Its 200,000 gallons contained a wide variety of Caribbean reef fish, including Morays,

Barracudas, Bonnethead Sharks and Sea Turtles. A variety of other displays branched off from the main tank. In 2013, the Ocean Tank was renovated and remodeled.

Expansions followed. The Aquarium was limited by the rather small tract of land it was located on, so in 1974 a specially-built barge, named *Discovery*, was docked in Boston Harbor alongside the Aquarium as a floating stadium. It housed a 116,000 gallon dolphin pool and a 1,000-seat arena for marine mammal shows. In 1998 a new West Wing was added to the Aquarium building, which housed the Harbor Seal display.

Grander plans were also made, and they led to trouble. In 1988, the Aquarium announced that it would sell its current waterfront building and relocate to a much larger site in the Charlestown Navy yard (near the popular "Old Ironsides" dock), where it would build a new $150 million facility. It would have been the largest public Aquarium in the world. But this idea died in 1991 when the Aquarium was unable to find a buyer for its current site.

As an alternative, then, the Aquarium drew up plans to expand the existing building with two additional wings that would have doubled the exhibit area. It was expected to be completed by 2004. But this too ran into insurmountable difficulties as the post 9-11 economy declined and visitorship to the existing Aquarium fell. The expansion was cancelled. This left the Aquarium deep in debt and forced large cuts to the budget. The resulting decline in staff led the AZA to revoke its accreditation, and it wasn't until 2006 that the Aquarium was finally out of the red and regained its AZA certification. By 2007 the Aquarium was able to finance a $42 million renovation and expansion, which upgraded the Ocean Tank, added a new Blue Penguin display, and opened an exhibit which featured the various conservation efforts being financed and carried out by the institution. By this time the Aquarium was receiving 1.3 million guests a year.

One of the most popular of the Aquarium's attractions, however, is not on display in a tank. The Aquarium runs regular tour boats out into the Atlantic Ocean to view one of the largest animals in North America—the Right Whale.

For over a century it was thought that all the Right Whales belonged to the same wide-ranging species, but modern DNA analysis has demonstrated that there are three distinct species. The Southern Right Whale is found across the southern hemisphere, while the Northern Right Whales are split into Atlantic and Pacific species. All three were hunted almost to extinction by 19th century whalers: they were eagerly pursued as the "right whales to hunt" because they tended to stay near shore, they floated when killed (making them easy to retrieve), and their thick blubber yielded large amounts of oil.

At one time, the Pygmy Right Whale, from the southern hemisphere, was considered a closely related species. Modern study has, however, indicated that it is not a Right Whale at all. It may be a surviving member of the Cetotheriid family — a group which was thought to be extinct.

Right Whales belong to a group called "baleen whales". These include some of the largest animals on earth, including Blue Whales. But these giants feed on tiny prey. Using rows of flexible fringed plates in their mouth called baleen or whalebone, they gulp in enormous amounts of seawater that contain planktonic copepods, small fish, and tiny shrimplike creatures called Krill, and filter out all the edibles.

As with all whales, reproduction is slow, which limits the ability of populations to rebound after being reduced. Mating usually occurs in the spring in the southern parts of the range. The pregnant females return north to feed, then migrate to the southern calving grounds the following year. The young are about 15 feet long when born and stay with their mothers for at least a year. Typically, a female will bear one calf every 3-5 years. The migrating whales and their calves tend to stay in shallower water close to shore in order to avoid hunting packs of Orcas.

Little is known about the lifespan of Right Whales. One solid data point was an individual adult female who was photographed in 1935 with a calf, and subsequently identified in photographs taken up until 1995, making her over 60 years old, perhaps as old as 80 or 90.

In 1980, researchers from the New England Aquarium discovered a previously-unknown migratory path being used by the Northern Atlantic Right Whales (*Eubalaena glacialis*), running from Canada to Georgia and passing at the Bay of Fundy and Cape Cod Bay. Believed at the time to be virtually extinct, the Whales were tracked by researchers, who found that there are around 400 Northern Atlantic Right Whales off the North American coast.

Spearheaded by the Aquarium's research, wildlife organizations successfully lobbied the Canadian and American governments to impose restrictions on shipping in order to clear ocean traffic away from the areas where the whales were congregating. This helped to prevent boat collisions, which, now that commercial whaling has ended, are one of the primary causes of deaths for these animals. The two nations also established the Stellwagen Bank National Marine Sanctuary in a rich feeding area about 30 miles offshore.

The Aquarium's research staff continues to study the Right Whales. Since the patterns of calluses on their skin are unique to each individual, photographs can be used to identify particular animals, and satellite tracking of GPS-tagged whales can follow their movements in real time.

Today, Aquarium guests are able to board a whale-watch excursion boat at the dockside and take the 4-hour trip out to the Stellwagen Bank area. Here they can observe a variety of species including Right Whales, Humpback Whales, Minke Whales, and Pilot Whales.

GEORGIA AQUARIUM
Atlanta GA

At the time it was built, the Georgia Aquarium was the largest in the world, and it remains as the largest in the US.

In 1979, two young men named Bernie Marcus and Arthur Blank were fired from the hardware store where they worked. Frustrated and angry, they decided to become business partners and open their own home improvement shop in Atlanta. They called it "Home Depot". By 2000, they were both multi-billionaires.

Marcus in particular became known for his philanthropy, donating money for children's medical research and at one point funding an emergency anthrax research lab at the Centers for Disease Control.

In 2001, Marcus announced that he would donate $250 million to the city of Atlanta for a public Aquarium, and to research the project, he visited 56 Aquariums in 13 different countries. The Coca-Cola company donated a 9-acre tract of land downtown, and other donors including AirTran Airways, BellSouth, Georgia-Pacific, Southern Company, SunTrust Bank, and Turner Broadcasting System, added $40 million in grants—enough to completely fund the construction and obtain the species collections. The Georgia Aquarium opened in November 2005, and reached a million visitors within its first 100 days. At 550,000 square feet, it remained the largest

Aquarium in the world until 2012, when bigger ones opened in Singapore and China.

The Aquarium was designed as five wings surrounding a central Atrium.

One of the areas was the Georgia Explorer, which displays various native species found in Georgia's saltwater and freshwater habitats. In 2015 this was expanded to include an exhibit of rescued California Sea Lions and was renamed Pier 225. The large school of Tarpon here were all rescued when they were stranded in a tidal pool on Skidaway Island off the Georgia coast.

Another gallery, known as Cold Water Quest, focuses on Arctic species and includes Puffins, Penguins and Spider Crabs. It is also home to a group of Belugas.

The River Scout area displays river species from around the world. There are Piranhas, Asian Small-Clawed Otters, Electric Eels, and others.

The Tropical Diver gallery holds a variety of reef tanks. There are thousands of fish here, most from the Indo-Pacific region. A large portion of them were captive-bred in commercial fish farms: a few of them were confiscated by Taiwanese authorities from illegal fishermen who caught them for the pet trade, and these were donated to the Aquarium. There are also a variety of seahorses, sea jellies, and shrimps.

The largest of the exhibits is called Ocean Voyager, which features animals from the Central American reefs such as Hammerhead Sharks, Stingrays, and Sawfish. One of the tanks here holds the Aquarium's Manta Rays. In 2008, a Manta Ray was rescued after becoming entangled in an anti-shark net off a beach in South Africa, and was sent to Atlanta, making the Georgia Aquarium one of only four places in the world to exhibit this species and the first to do so in North America. Other rescues followed, and by 2012 the Aquarium had four Manta Rays on exhibit.

The Ocean Voyager also contains the most unique species on exhibit at the Aquarium—the Whale Sharks.

Despite the name and immense size, the Whale Shark is not really a whale, but is the largest species of shark. Adult males have been measured at around 30 feet, and females at around 45 feet, though individuals up to 60 feet have been reported, making them some of the largest living species. Only some of the whale species get bigger.

Even though they are some of the most massive animals on earth, Whale Sharks were completely unknown to science until the 19th century and are still only poorly understood. In April 1828, a group of whalers harpooned a Whale Shark off the coast of South Africa. It was studied by a British doctor in Cape Town named Smith, who first described it in print and gave it the Latin name *Rhincodon typus*. The huge fish had the cartilaginous skeleton typically found in sharks, but unlike most sharks, which are fast sharp-toothed predators, the Whale Shark was a placid filter feeder, swimming along in the open ocean and gathering plankton, krill and small fish in its open mouth where a fringe on its gill arches strains food from the seawater.

The Whale Shark was eventually found to inhabit tropical waters worldwide, rarely venturing into areas where the water temperature was below 70F. It appears to be at least somewhat migratory, with yearly gatherings occurring in Mexico, South Africa, Mozambique, Australia, the Philippines and Taiwan.

It is known that the sharks give live birth, but their breeding and calving grounds are entirely unknown, though young Whale Sharks have been seen near the Philippines. Pregnant females have been found with up to 300 embryos in their body, but it appears they are not born all at once but are born several at a time over a long period. They seem to be around two feet long at birth. The embryos are not nourished by the female's body, but form inside their own egg cases which are retained until the young hatch and are born live. Studies of their skeleton indicate that adult Whale Sharks may live up to 50 years, perhaps as many as 80.

Despite their immense size, Whale Sharks are docile fish and pose no threat to humans. They sometimes allow human divers to interact with them. In some areas, such as Mexico, Australia and the Philippines, the Sharks have become popular tourist attractions for both divers and boats. In Asia, Whale Sharks have long been used for food (shark fin soup being an expensive delicacy) and also for "traditional Chinese medicine". A number of Sharks are also killed each year in collisions with ships. Although the population numbers are only poorly known, Whale Sharks have been given legal protections in many areas. The Philippines banned Whale Shark fishing in 1998, with India joining in 2001 and Taiwan in 2008. The species is also now listed in the Convention on International Trade in Endangered Species (CITES). There are indications that the population is declining: in some areas, the number of observed individuals seems to have decreased by 50% over the past 40 years, though it is not clear whether this is caused by falling population or by alterations in migratory patterns and feeding areas due to climate change. But as a precaution, since the species seems to reach sexual maturity at a late age and reproduces only slowly, the Whale Shark is now classed as "endangered" in the IUCN Red List.

In recent years, new technology like satellite tracking has allowed for increased scientific study of Whale Sharks. The conspicuous white spots on the Shark's back have patterns that are unique to each individual, allowing researchers to identify them by aerial photos, sometimes using computer software that was designed for astronomers to recognize star patterns. (There are now websites that allow tourists to submit vacation photos of Whale Sharks so they can be identified by their spot patterns, allowing the individual fish's movements to be tracked). Electronic tags that measure depth have shown that some Whale Sharks occasionally make deep dives, up to 6,000 feet. No one knows why. Other GPS tags have shown that the huge fish sometimes swim as much as 5,000 miles over a period of 4 or 5 months, and again nobody knows why.

The first public Aquarium to attempt to keep Whale Sharks in captive conditions was in Okinawa in the 1980s, when a series of stranded individuals and a few that had been accidentally caught in fishing nets were brought to the Churaumi Aquarium for rehabilitation. Some of these were released successfully after a time, but overall the survival rate in captivity was low. Maintaining Whale Sharks in captivity is difficult because of the specialized feeding habits and the extraordinarily large tanks that are necessary. As Churaumi gained more experience, however, the survival rate went up: one Whale Shark was successfully kept for almost 20 years. Learning from these experiences, other Asian Aquariums began taking in rescued Whale Sharks as well, in Japan, China, India, Korea and Taiwan. The Georgia Aquarium is the first institution outside of Asia to attempt to maintain Whale Sharks in captivity.

The Aquarium specifically intended from the beginning to keep rescued Whale Sharks, with a 6.3-million gallon display tank constructed as a centerpiece. At the time the tank was built, Taiwan was allowing fishermen to take a specified number of Whale Sharks per year for sale as food—and the Aquarium agreed to buy four of these, alive. The four young Sharks, named Ralph, Norton, Alice, and Trixie, were carefully shipped to Atlanta by air, boat and truck. Unfortunately two of them died after a time, and were replaced by two new rescues. Another one died in 2020. The Aquarium works closely with the Asian institutions on research and conservation, to learn more about these animals both in captivity and in the wild.

In addition to the Whale Sharks, the Aquarium is heavily involved in other conservation projects. Georgia Aquarium has partnered with Sea World, the Shedd Aquarium and Vancouver Aquarium to captive-breed Belugas as part of the species protection program. In order to expand the gene pool for their Belugas, this group applied for a permit to import 18 individuals from Russia, but the US National Marine Fisheries Service denied permission, saying that they did not want to encourage the Russians to begin capturing wild Belugas and selling them.

The Aquarium has also worked with several institutions, including Georgia Tech, the University of the South Pacific in Fiji, and the State of Florida to research coral-bleaching diseases that threaten tropical reefs, and to research ways to propagate its own coral for use in its exhibit tanks.

In 2010, the Dolphin Coast gallery was opened. This $100-million expansion features a stadium for educational dolphin shows as well as displays and exhibits. In 2011, the Aquarium purchased Marineland, an aging tourist attraction in Florida that featured performing dolphins, and transformed it into a rescue center for sea turtles and marine mammals. The Aquarium now carries out research on wild dolphin populations in the southeastern US.

Since its opening in 2005, the Aquarium has added several new exhibits. The Aquanaut Adventure: A Discovery Zone contains hands-on displays and touch tanks for kids. In 2020, the Aquarium opened a new gallery titled "Sharks! Predators of the Deep", which features educational exhibits and conservation information about the world's shark species. A display tank contains Hammerhead Sharks, Sand Tiger Sharks, Tiger Sharks, Zebra Sharks, and others, and for a fee visitors can enter a dive cage inside the tank.

AQUARIUM OF THE PACIFIC
Long Beach CA

In 1990, the Disney company was looking to expand its California attractions. The "Disney Decade" plan called for a second park to be added at Disneyland, which would eventually open as "California Adventure". But there were also plans for a brand-new complex in Long Beach, to be called "Port Disney".

When Disneyland was constructed in 1955, there was not enough money in the budget for the company to both build the park and construct its own hotels around it, so Disney invited several businessmen to finance and build hotels next to Disney property. One of these was Jack Wrather, who, with Disney's cooperation, built and managed the Disney Hotel.

The park turned out to be an enormous success, and after a short time Disney offered to buy out all of the private owners whom it had invited in. But Wrather refused to sell, and continued to run the Disney Hotel until his death in 1988. All of Wrather's various properties were then put up for sale, and Disney eagerly snatched them up. As it happened, one of the properties that Wrather had held was the 55-acre patch of land in Long Beach where the retired cruise ship *Queen Mary* was docked as a floating hotel and the Howard Hughes airplane "Spruce Goose" was being exhibited.

This purchase offered the opportunity for a second Disney attraction in California, and the company went all-out in its plans. The 55-acre Long Beach site would be expanded by dredging the shoreline and building up another 250 acres of newly-claimed land by piling up sand and fill. "Port Disney" would include a terminal for the Disney cruise line, and also a state-of-the art ocean research lab and a futuristic Aquarium to be called "DisneySea". There would be a boardwalk, five Disney-owned hotels, artificial beaches, and a variety of rides and pavilions based on sea legends. The entire project was estimated at $3 billion.

In the end, however, the massive undertaking proved to be too much even for Disney's swollen checkbook. The ecologically-sensitive California coastline is heavily protected by a slew of local, state, and federal regulations, and the budget soon swelled out of sight. Before the dredging operation had even been started, Disney pulled the plug on the project. A mini-version of "DisneySea" would later be built in Disney Tokyo, but by December 1991 the California venture was dead.

It was a huge disappointment to the city of Long Beach, which had been looking forward to the flood of tourist dollars that Disney would have provided, and also saw the project as a way to revitalize a waterfront area that was now largely empty after the US Navy closed its nearby Naval Station and Shipyard. But Mayor Beverly O'Neill liked the idea of an Aquarium, and Disney's market research had already indicated that it would be popular with the public. An engineering study also decided that it would be feasible to dredge new land at the site. So, the city adopted part of Disney's idea and set up a $185 million fund to finance it.

The Aquarium of the Pacific opened in June 1998. There were three large exhibit galleries. The Southern Pacific wing features the 142,000-gallon Blue Cavern tank, which contains species native to the Catalina Islands, and the Amber Forest tank with a live Giant Kelp forest. There is also a Sea Lion Pool, a Stingray touchtank, and a seabird rescue center. The Northern Pacific gallery displays species from the Bering Sea area around Alaska. There are Sea Otters, Octopus, and Spider Crabs. The Tropical Pacific gallery is built around the 350,000-

gallon Reef Tank which contains fish from the Palau coral reefs as well as Sea Turtles.

Other galleries and displays include Shark Lagoon, Lorikeet Forest, and the Penguin Habitat. In the main lobby is a life-size fiberglass model whale and her calf. In 2019, the Aquarium added the $53 million Pacific Visions wing, which focuses on education and outreach using interactive displays and exhibits. "It's non-traditional for an Aquarium because most Aquariums that would expand would be building bigger tanks for bigger animals," Aquarium President Dr Jerry Schubel said of the new addition. "This will have some animals in it. But the one animal that is putting everyone at risk on this planet is you and me."

One of the animals that the Aquarium's conservation message focuses on is the White Abalone.

Abalone are a group of marine snails in the Haliotid family. There is only one genus, *Haliotis*, and the number of species runs from 57 to almost 100 depending on whether you are a lumper or a splitter. These ocean mollusks can be found in tropical and temperate seas around the world.

In appearance they are all similar, with shells in the form of a flattened spiral ranging in size from barely an inch to almost a foot. There is a series of holes along the outer rim, which are used to push water in and out for breathing. The shell is made of tiny plates of calcium carbonate held together by a protein matrix.

Most of the shell's interior is taken up by the foot. Marine snails have only one foot, which is large and powerful. By protruding the foot and sliding along, the Abalone is able to move, but it spends most of its time in one spot, clinging to rocks in the intertidal zone. The grip is very strong, both to prevent the mollusk from being washed away by a wave and to prevent predators from prying the animal off. The body cavity also contains the heart, stomach and other organs. Water is passed in and out over the gills, allowing the snail to extract oxygen. One oddity is that Abalones do not have any clotting factors in their blood, so even a tiny cut can prove fatal to them.

Abalones are herbivores and feed by scraping algae and plant material using a raspy toothed tongue called a "radula".

There are seven Abalone species found in California waters: Black, White, Red, Green, Pink, Flat, and Pinto. Three of these are protected under the Endangered Species Act, and the rarest is the White Abalone, *Haliotis sorenseni*, which in 2001 became the first marine mollusk to be federally listed. This is a deepwater species that prefers depths of at least 80 feet and sometimes as deep as 200 feet. It is often found in Kelp Forest habitat, where it grazes on algae and helps thin out the Kelp so new stalks can grow.

The outer shell of most Abalones is drab and looks like a rock, but the inside of the shell is lined with shimmering and iridescent "mother of pearl". The spectacular shell is highly prized in many cultures and has been used for decoration and jewelry since caveman times. Glittering pieces of shell that were drilled for a necklace have been found in Paleolithic sites, and even in modern times Abalone mother-of-pearl has been used to make buttons and as colorful inlays for woodworking. Some native cultures around the world have used the shells as money. Like Oysters, Abalone also sometimes remove an irritant inside their shells by coating it with iridescent layers to form a pearl, and these are highly valued by jewelry-makers.

The flesh of the Abalone, which consists mostly of the muscular foot, is also highly sought by humans and has long been considered a delicacy. In China, Abalone meat is known as *bao yu*, and has traditionally been served as a luxury item for special occasions such as weddings. In the US west coast, roasted and discarded Abalone shell is common in Native American midden piles dating back over 12,000 years. Today, Abalone meat is sometimes found as a luxury west coast pizza topping.

According to local legend, the California Abalone industry began in 1900 when a German immigrant named Doelter, piqued that his shipment of Oysters were always late, sought out a local alternative and found it in the Abalones that grew wild in Monterey Bay. After pounding the meat to tenderize it, Doelter coated it with crumbs and fried it in butter. It was an instant hit. By the 1930s, warehouses in Cannery Row were pouring out tins of canned Abalone as well as sardines. Worldwide, millions of pounds of Abalone were being taken each year.

It was simply unsustainable, and populations began to drop. As the snails got harder to find, the price went up, which encouraged people to look harder. By the 1950s, many species of Abalone were virtually extinct in the wild

That, in turn, led to commercial farming. Like many other marine creatures, Abalones do not mate directly, but instead they will all, responding to some environmental cue, release their eggs and sperm into the water at the same time. When they find each other, these reproductive cells form tiny larvae which drift in the tide for a while before settling on the bottom, growing a shell, and turning into miniature Abalones.

Abalone farm operators would raise larvae in indoors tanks until they were big enough to release outside in a shallow patch of artificial reef on a shoreline: the adults were then harvested when they reached suitable size. Today most of the market is being supplied by commercial Abalone farms in China, Japan and Korea, and the harvesting of wild Abalones is illegal or restricted.

All of the Abalones, however, are still threatened or endangered. Wild populations have become legally protected and more of the food supply is met by farm-raised mollusks, but the global population continues to decline. One of the side effects of rising CO_2 levels and ocean temperatures is a higher level of dissolved carbon dioxide in the seawater, which makes it slightly acid instead of the normally neutral pH. This acidic water attacks the calcium carbonate that makes up most mollusk shells, leading to weakened and dead animals.

The rising temperatures also have led to the spread of a warm-water bacteria that causes "withering syndrome", a fatal disease which causes a mollusk's esophagus to become infected. The animal stops eating, weakens, and succumbs as the bacteria spreads through its body organs.

A number of state and federal agencies have attempted to stabilize the population of Abalone by using some of the same farming techniques developed by commercial growers to release hand-raised youngsters into the sea. Most of these species, however, are only poorly understood: there have never been many biologists who specialized in studying them, and now that they are virtually gone there are no longer many wild Abalones left to study.

On the whole, then, most of these conservation efforts have been of only limited effect, since they cannot correct the underlying environmental issues (acidification and seawater warming) that have caused the Abalone populations to stagnate. Some studies have concluded that, at current rates of decline, Abalones will be entirely extinct by the 24th century.

CLEARWATER MARINE AQUARIUM

Clearwater FL

The nonprofit Clearwater Marine Aquarium in Clearwater FL has been doing marine mammal, bird, and turtle rescue work since the mid-1980's, after the city donated an old water treatment plant which was modified into holding tanks for rescued animals.

In 1972, a group of local citizens formed the Clearwater Marine Science Center as a nonprofit organization. Hoping to do rescue work for local marine life, they approached the City of Clearwater about obtaining the old water treatment plant — with its large cement water tanks, it was perfectly suited for keeping and quarantining aquatic animals. After several years of remodeling, the Center received all of their necessary State and Federal permits, and the Clearwater Marine Aquarium opened to the public.

More of a working marine hospital than an exhibit Aquarium, the center began to rescue, rehabilitate and release injured and distressed marine wildlife. Those animals which could not be released for various reasons (including Dolphins, Sea Turtles, River Otters and Pelicans) were placed on exhibit for use in educational shows and as a way to raise funds for the hospital operations through admission tickets.

The Center's first permanent resident was a beached Bottlenose Dolphin named "Sunset Sam", who was rescued in 1984. As part of his enrichment program, Sam was taught how to paint on a canvas, and his paintings were then sold at auction to help finance the rescue operations.

For years, the center was barely making ends meet.

In 2006, the Aquarium took in a young rescued female dolphin who had become entangled in a crab trap and had lost her tail. Because it was December, the staff named her "Winter".

Without her tail, Winter could not swim properly—not only could she not be released back to the wild, but it was doubtful she would survive at all. But on her own, Winter learned to swim again, by moving her tail stump side to side like a fish instead of up and down like a dolphin. Unfortunately, this produced bad effects on the spinal column, and it was decided to try to fit Winter with a prosthetic tail. After much research and trial and error a workable prosthetic was made, which is now fitted on Winter several hours a day to allow her to swim properly and exercise, and ease the strain on her spine and muscles. Winter became a well-known local attraction.

Then in 2010, Hollywood came calling. A division of Warner Brothers approached the Aquarium with an offer to make a movie about Winter. In exchange, Warner Brothers agreed to finance a full remodeling and expansion of the Aquarium building, adding new exhibits like the Stingray Touch Tank, a new tank for dolphin shows, and several new rescue tanks. "Dolphin Tale", starring Morgan Freeman, Ashley Judd, Harry Connick Jr, and Kris Kristofferson, opened in 2011. Nearly the entire movie was shot on location at the Aquarium. With the publicity from the movie and increased attendance, the Aquarium was able to expand its rescue, rehabilitation, and education work. In 2012, the Aquarium was able to open a second building in downtown Clearwater devoted to the movie, with behind the scenes exhibits and props used in the filming.

Meanwhile, the Aquarium obtained another dolphin celebrity. In December 2010, rescuers found a stranded Bottlenose Dolphin at Indian River Lagoon, and a 2-month old calf who was still trying to nurse from her dead mother. The calf was taken to the Aquarium and named "Hope". She was successfully rehabilitated, but because of her young age she had not been able to learn how to live in the wild before she was orphaned, and cannot be released. Hope's story was the inspiration for another Hollywood movie, "Dolphin Tale 2", which was also filmed on location at the Aquarium and released in 2014. The sequel film also featured a Sea Turtle named "Mavis", which was actually a rescued turtle named "Harold", a permanent resident of the Aquarium who was found in 2010 wandering on a beach. He suffers from neurological disorders that limit his eyesight, making him unreleasable.

All of the other animals at the Aquarium are also rescues. There are two Nurse Sharks, named Thelma and Louise, which had been illegally taken from the wild by a collector as youngsters. There are a large number of Sea Turtles, including Loggerheads, Green Sea Turtles, and Kemp's Ridley Sea Turtles. Most of these were hit by boats. And there are two North American River Otters named Boomer and Walle, and four White Pelicans. But most of the Aquarium's work revolves around Florida's Atlantic Bottlenose Dolphins.

There are about 40 different species of Dolphin, all in the family Delphinidae. They are mammals, not fish, and are closely related to the whales. The fossil record shows that Dolphins are some of the most recent whales to have evolved, appearing only within the past 9-10 million years. In that time they have diversified to fill nearly every available aquatic habitat, from shallow tropical seas to ice-filled Arctic oceans to large freshwater rivers.

The Atlantic Spotted Dolphin and the European Common Dolphin can sometimes be found in Florida's coastal waters, but by far the most often-encountered is the Atlantic Bottlenose Dolphin (*Tursiops truncatus*). This species is familiar to everyone from its many TV and movie appearances, from "Flipper" to "Dolphin Tale". The Bottlenose Dolphin is about ten feet long, blueish-gray on top and whitish below. The males can be recognized by the two distinct slits in their bellies; the females have only one. The species is found throughout most of the world's oceans, from as far north as Norway to as far south as South Africa. In the Indian Ocean it is replaced by the Indo-Pacific Bottlenose, *Turciops aduncus*, and the dolphins near Melbourne, Australia, are classified as the Burrunan Bottlenose, *Tursiops australis*. DNA analysis shows some differences between the Atlantic populations that live near the coastlines and those which prefer the deeper ocean, and there are also some physical differences in size and coloring: it is possible that they are two distinct species and are reproductively isolated. Some taxonomists also class the Pacific Bottlenose Dolphin as a separate species, *Turciops gillis*.

Sometimes dolphins are referred to as a "porpoise", but the true porpoises are a separate biological family.

Dolphins are very long-lived animals. Wild Bottlenose Dolphins have been observed at fifty years, though the typical lifespan seems to be around 25-30. The females also seem to be capable of breeding for virtually their entire adult lives. The young are born live after a pregnancy of 12 months, and the calf then stays with its mother for up to 5 years, reaching sexual maturity at around age 10, though this can vary according to gender and geography. Bottlenose Dolphins have been known to hybridize with a number of other Dolphin species, both in captivity and in the wild.

What makes Dolphins so interesting to humans, though, is their extraordinary level of intelligence. The Encephalization Quotient (the ratio of brain size to body mass) in Dolphins is one of the highest in the animal kingdom. They are also highly social, living in "pods" of up to 20 individuals. The females tend to congregate in groups called "bands", while adult males tend to form cooperative pairs. Bottlenose Dolphins can often be seen hunting cooperatively, with one or two individuals herding a school of fish up against a seawall or other obstacle to allow another individual to dart in and catch the prey before changing places. At one fishing village in Brazil, the Dolphins have learned to signal to the fishing boats where to cast their nets, so they can prey on the panicked fish that manage to escape. This particular pod has been passing down this behavior to its young for over 150 years. Dolphins in Australia have also been observed using sea sponges plucked from rocks as tools to hunt in the bottom muck.

While Bottlenose Dolphins have excellent hearing and eyesight, like all Dolphins they experience their world mostly through echolocation. By sending out a series of high-frequency clicks through a fatty organ in their forehead called the "melon", they are able to read the echoes through their teeth and jawbones like sonar, and seem to be able to detect detailed sonogram images of obstacles, other Dolphins, prey, and potential predators. Although a dolphin's echolocation clicks are one of the loudest sounds made by any animal, they happen at a frequency too high for human ears to detect. Each individual has its own "signature whistle" that refers to itself, and the Dolphins all communicate with each other through a series of squeaks and squeals, some of them audible to humans. These sounds are produced by the nasal opening at the top of the head, known as the "blowhole".

In most areas, Bottlenose Dolphins have few natural predators, though large sharks or Orcas occasionally eat them. (Dolphins have very effective immune systems and can usually survive bites and injuries that would kill most other animals.) In Japan, Dolphins are eaten as food, usually in the form of raw *sashimi*, but the primary danger to Dolphins from humans comes from net fishing, which often entangles and drowns the air-breathing mammals. Today fisheries are required to use nets which are designed to allow Dolphins to escape. All dolphins and whales are protected by the Marine Mammals Act.

Virtually every coastal town in Florida has "dolphin boats" which take tourists out to watch the Dolphins. There are also a number of Aquariums, like Sea World and Marineland, which have captive Dolphins on display and sometimes allow human interaction with them.

The practice of keeping captive Dolphins has, however, generated a lot of controversy as many have argued that intelligent and social species like Dolphins should not be confined in captivity. Many Zoos and Aquariums have been giving up their Dolphin displays. In the Keys, by contrast, there are places where wild Bottlenose Dolphins, drawn by curiosity and playfulness, voluntarily enter into shallow coves to interact with humans.

In 2020 the Clearwater Aquarium underwent another expansion to increase its capacity. The dolphin rescue facilities were tripled in size to 1.5 million gallons, and the hospital and education areas have also been enlarged. A new Visitor's Center was added, as well as additional visitor parking.

PHOTO ALBUM

Emus

Sulawesi Macaque

Orangutan

Ruffed Lemur

African Crowned Crane

Harpy Eagle

Fossa

Green Mamba

White Rhino

Banded Sunfish

Sun Bear

Poison Dart Frog

Giant Panda

Komodo Dragon

Lesser Flamingo

Rhinoceros Hornbill

Chimpanzee

Fennec Fox

Knobtailed Gecko

Northern Tree Shrew

Blue Tree Monitor

Red Panda

Made in United States
Troutdale, OR
12/20/2025